To Ruth + Dwight:

For your birthdays
of 1975

Love,

Dad + Mother J.

LANDSCAPE

LANDSCAPE

a bundle of thoughts about the Psalms
(the first fifty)

G. TH. ROTHUIZEN
TRANSLATED BY JOHN FREDERICK JANSEN

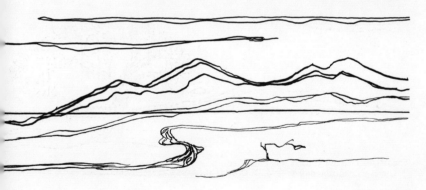

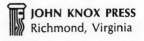

JOHN KNOX PRESS
Richmond, Virginia

The original Dutch edition was published under the title *Landschap*.
© Uitgeversmaatschappij J. H. Kok N.V. Kampen, Holland, 1965.

Unless otherwise indicated, Scripture quotations are from the *Revised Standard Version of the Bible,* copyrighted 1946 and 1952.

International Standard Book Number: 0-8042-2405-6
Library of Congress Catalog Card Number: 70-133241
© M. E. Bratcher 1971
Printed in the United States of America

To A. A. van Ruler

CONTENTS

TRANSLATOR'S PREFACE

No one can gainsay what the Psalms have meant to the faith and life of Israel and the church. One can question whether the church is sufficiently aware of the Psalter's rich resources for the living of these days. Oddly enough, while our liturgical renewal acknowledges the central place of the Psalter, it has done little to secure a more central place for the Psalms in hymnal and lectionary. And what is true of corporate worship is also true of private use. For many Christians the Psalter has been reduced to a few favorite Psalms, and these are often more tinged with sentiment than translated into present testimony.

That is why I count it a pleasure to introduce this unusual volume to a larger circle of readers—not only because the author is from a church tradition in which psalmody is still the heart of hymnody, but also because his fresh and vigorous insights can do much to quicken our own appreciation and appropriation of the Psalms.

The present volume contains "thoughts" about the first fifty Psalms. Instead of picking and choosing a few favorites, as though others are either too distant or too difficult to speak to us today, it is a rewarding experience to be led through the Psalms seriatim, and to discover how surprisingly and refreshingly the word of the Bible is the word for today.

Again, over against the frequent disposition to separate the secular from the sacred, the temporal from the eternal, the doctrinal from the ethical, these studies (as the Psalms to which they point us) are imbued with social awareness and ethical urgency. An articulate ethic needs an articulate theology, and these are inseparable in the biblical word.

Finally, these studies can help us appreciate anew that biblical exposition is the most immediate, indispensable, and rewarding activity for anyone who takes his faith and his world seriously. No one who reads these pages will be disposed to think that such study is drab or dull. The author brings the biblical word to the present with candor and humor and hope.

Dr. Rothuizen is professor of ethics in the Theological School of the Reformed Churches of the Netherlands at Kampen. Recently he has published a very informative volume on Dietrich Bonhoeffer.

American readers will not be familiar with the commentaries of J. Ridderbos and of his son, N. H. Ridderbos, to which frequent allusion is made. Other commentaries may not express as much confidence in the traditional ascriptions of Davidic authorship and context. No matter. Our author is less concerned with speculating about a Psalm's origin than he is with bringing this Psalm to the present scene. Again, if the memory of the Second War is beginning to fade for some of us, the memories of Nazi occupation and especially of the slaughter of the Jews remain very much alive in these studies. Nor does this make the book any less contemporary. If Dr. Rothuizen points to the issues of race, armaments, international tensions, Far East, etc., in terms of his Dutch milieu, we can and must transpose these to the racial crisis in our country, to the recent debate about ABM, and to the tragic conflict in Indochina. If the shoe fits!

Let me express my appreciation to the author for his careful reading of an earlier draft of this translation and for his helpful corrections and suggestions. Let me also express appreciation to the secretaries of Austin Presbyterian Theological Seminary who graciously typed the final draft of the translation: Mrs. Jack Howard, Miss Sharon Alexander, and Mrs. Lane Allen.

JOHN FREDERICK JANSEN

BY WAY OF INTRODUCTION

These comments on the Psalms first appeared in the *Centraal Weekblad,* a periodical published for the Gereformeerden Kerken in the Netherlands. When the first fifty had appeared, the publisher asked me to make them available for a collected volume—an invitation I accepted gladly.

I'm indebted to Mr. Henk Krijger for the title of the volume. I think the title speaks for itself. It wants to portray with a single comment the total climate of our human existence, in its height and depth, as one that is waiting for the Lord. This line of Charles (pseudonym for Professor W. H. Nagel which originated during the time of the occupation and has continued for his literary work), taken as a motto, is the first line of his poem *Melle*— a poem which has remarkable affinities with the world of the Psalms.

I spoke of "comments on the Psalms." What follows, however, does not pretend to offer actual commentary. Intentionally there is too much free rein of thought for that. Sometimes they were sermons, sometimes a sort of meditation. What they are actually I don't really know. Perhaps that is why the whole is best described as "thoughts about."

Finally, let me dedicate these thoughts to Professor A. A. van Ruler, professor of theology at the University of Utrecht, whose own scriptural meditations (as indeed all of his theology) have always been for me a source of joy and strength. Nor can I conclude this introduction to the American edition without a word of appreciation to the publisher, who must have some confidence in its appearance. Let me express appreciation also to the translator, Professor Jansen of the Austin Presbyterian Theological Seminary. I can imagine a Dutch which is easier to translate than mine! I think he has done a very fine job and one with which I am altogether satisfied.

G. TH. ROTHUIZEN

"This is the landscape that awaits the Lord . . ."

J. B. CHARLES

LIKE A TREE

"He is like a tree . . ."

—Psalm 1:3

It's not difficult to see why someone might find Psalm 1 a quite insufferable Psalm about a quite insufferable fellow. There he sits, day and night, brooding and fretting over the law. What a pedant! Or worse. Isn't such a person called a Pharisee in the New Testament? Accordingly, must we not say, what a Pharisee? Doesn't this become plain in the antithesis which tells us not to be "there" (in the counsel of the wicked, in the way of sinners, in the seat of scoffers), but "here" (near the law)? Can't we hear the Pharisee of the New Testament saying, "God, I thank thee that I am not like other men, extortioners, unjust, adulterers," etc. (Luke 18:11)? And that Pharisee did not get off too well. What, then, would Jesus have said about the man in Psalm 1, and about the lines of division drawn by him and around him? Didn't He break through precisely these divisions when the Pharisees said to His disciples, "Why does your teacher eat with tax collectors and sinners" (Matt. 9:11)? Can we not say—must we not say—how insufferable, how *boring,* is our Psalm's portrayal when compared with our Savior's way of doing?

A wrong view

Shall we quickly say that we ought not talk like this? No. After all, if *in* the Psalms people are allowed to say a good deal about rebellion, resentment, doubt—then surely we're allowed to say a good deal *about* the Psalms, particularly when we're at a loss as to what to do with them in terms of the gospel. Nonetheless, that doesn't mean that this particular view of our Psalm is necessarily correct.

In general it's safe to say that when we are in the vicinity of the law (and that includes the Psalms), we are not in the vicinity of what is irksome, barren, and dry. After all, the law is described as honey, "sweeter also than honey" (Ps. 19:10)! That has nothing to do with oppressive anxiety. Quite the contrary. God's law is unlimited (Ps. 119:96). It is more like an unlimited vacation trip. And there's music in it (Ps. 119:54)! Indeed, the law is like a wedding, the most festive imaginable—and more (Ps. 19:5)!

If in general the law has nothing in common with narrowness or with narrow people, this is particularly true of our Psalm. The "climate" of one who is absorbed in the law is like that of a tree planted by streams of water. That sounds hale and hearty. That's dynamic rather than static. Indeed, words like "static" or "dynamic" scarcely apply here. At any rate, it all sounds unbelievably fruitful.

Antithesis

Speaking of fruitfulness, what is meant by this should be clear enough. We know what it means from the teaching of Jesus who uses the image of the tree and its fruits in the Sermon on the Mount (Matt. 7:17-20). For that matter, He makes use of other material from our Psalm in that Sermon. We recall the familiar two ways (vs. 6) which we meet again in Matthew 7:13-14. To walk in the right way, to be fruitful, means not to walk alone but to be something for one's neighbor rather than to live for oneself alone.

What is meant by the wicked, the sinners, and the scoffers now becomes clear. We must not identify them too quickly with those whom today we call atheists—the followers of Multatuli or of Nietzsche, the enthusiasts of Vestdijk's *The Future of Religion,* or the Bolsheviks in Moscow. No. We're concerned here with a group-

ing and an antithesis *within* the chosen people, within Israel, of
which apparently not all are "Israel" (Rom. 9:6). The wicked are
the unfruitful, those who are indifferent to neighbor. They are the
evildoers, those who speak lies, the "bloodthirsty and deceitful
men" (Ps. 5:6). All this fits an image in our Psalm which we
meet again in the New Testament—the image of chaff. John the
Baptist uses this image in his teaching, along with the image of
the tree (Matt. 3:10, 12). He uses it explicitly again when ad-
dressing those who shortchange their neighbor (Luke 3:9-14, 17).

There is indeed an antithesis. But it's the antithesis between the
vital tree and the dry chaff. It's the antithesis of what is fruitful
and what is unfruitful. Moreover, in this image discipline comes
into view. The church must be such that self-seekers no longer
will be able to abide in it and, in the name of God, will simply be
driven out of it. Conversely, no Christian can prosper in unneighborly relationships—whether in the church, in the state, or in society at large. In his commentary, J. Ridderbos observes that we
must not think of separation in the sense of pharisaic Judaism.
Rather, we must think of separation from the world as the apostle
John understands this. John does not keep us guessing as to what
he means by "world" or "worldly." He means the world of lovelessness. That's what his whole first epistle is all about. Whoever
practices lovelessness commits idolatry (1 John 5:21). In short,
whoever is indifferent to his neighbor is the wicked or ungodly
man.

Astonishing

Does that mean that an upright man prospers in all he does?
That's what it says! Once again, we must distinguish carefully.
The men of the Psalms knew all too well that fruitfulness is not
the same as success. We recall the complaint of Asaph. The men
of the Psalms were painfully aware of the difference between
fruitfulness and success. We need not wait for what we call the
new covenant to learn this. Conversely, we must not suppose
that the typical wisdom teaching of the Old Testament which says
"who does good meets good" is out of date. Bonhoeffer is right.

The New Testament teaches no cross without blessing, and the Old Testament teaches no blessing without cross. If we are to interpret verse 3 of our Psalm it's well to think of verse 1 of Psalm 23. Even though a man is face to face with the valley of the shadow of death, he shall not want if the Lord is his shepherd—that is, if he clings to this Lord. Such a man knows his way, his direction, his destiny—whereas another will lose his way. Now we can see how the other loses his way—in his own lovelessness.

Here we ought to pause. This is truly astonishing. God calls my way a *way*! Ordinarily, one wouldn't say this. When my way is directed toward the neighbor, doesn't it often seem impractical and thankless? Moreover, it's astonishing for another and a deeper reason. Who am I—that I can be fruitful, that I can mean something for someone else? Astonishing!

And humorous

No wonder that what follows might be called a bit humorous. The strong fellow described "like a tree" in our Psalm through all this becomes as tiny as a child. It's as though he hears Jesus say, ". . . unless you turn and become like children" (Matt. 18:3) you cannot become like a tree. Nor need he wait to hear the beatitudes in the New Testament to realize that, already in the Old Testament, the "blessed" addressed to the man who is like a tree (vs. 1) only applies to one who knows "Blessed are the poor in spirit, the meek, the merciful, the pure, the peacemakers." That's how he becomes such a strong fellow—in poverty of spirit, in meekness, in mercy, in purity, in love of peace (Ps. 37).

Isn't it difficult to be "like a tree"? No. One only needs to have faith like a mustard seed (Matt. 17:20). That is, one only need understand a little something about it and, lo, a tree arises in which the birds of the air make their nests (Matt. 13:32). That's something that can be seen!

Let's ask the question again. Is it difficult to be like a tree? Answer: ask a tree. A tree won't understand such a question at all—of course not. The life of the faithful is incomprehensibly self-evident.

BONDS

*"Kiss the Son, lest he be angry,
and ye perish from the way . . ."*

—Psalm 2:12 (K.J.V.)

The second Psalm is also concerned with the wicked. Their lawlessness is wickedness. Their way leads nowhere. The difference between this Psalm and the first is that here we do not meet these wicked men directly within the chosen people but among the nations of the world. We notice a further comparison. If the man of Psalm 1 is busy day and night meditating on God's law, the men of Psalm 2 are also busy meditating about something. It doesn't get them anywhere, however, for it is a "meditating about vanity." In Hebrew, the same word is used in both instances. But how different in practice!

God's derision

How does God react to the vain goings-on of the world's braggards who are trying to grab His crown? We read: "He who sits in the heavens laughs." That is to say, He who resides at a distance eternally secure from all the aggression directed against Him, laughs. It's as though He says, "Try it if you dare. You can't reach Me!" The Lord has them in derision. The worst part of that derision is not even the deriding but the absolute ignoring. That's the worst thing one person can do to another—and that God can do to men. And yet, that such derision still wants to express itself is actually redemptive. This God, as we read in verse 5, is still willing to be angry. He is still willing to trouble Himself, to be angry, and to terrify them in His fury. He still wants to be heard. Apparently, He's still willing to *look* at us!

The ideal king

What else do we hear? We discover that something can be done besides what the kings in our Psalm do. There are other kings, there is an anointed of the Lord to whom God has said, "You are my son."

We are reminded of 2 Samuel 7:14: "I will be his father, and he shall be my son." The words make us think of an actual, historical king. Yet, to say this is not enough. In Israel's history no king known to us has stood so manfully against a hostile world as is the case here. Accordingly, we have to think of an "ideal" king. For that matter, all nations have tried to see their kings as ideal, even as sons of the gods. Well, our poet says, the king we dream about is not one bit less. Quite the contrary! In the Old Testament world, of course, men did not think of Jesus Christ in this connection, whereas in the New Testament world of course men thought of Him. This is already evident in Acts 4:27. There the conspiracy of which we read in the Psalm is interpreted as a conspiracy against Jesus (cf. Acts 13:33; Heb. 1:5; 5:5; Rev. 2:27; 19:15).

The modest judgment

How shall we read this Psalm today? To begin, let's look at those kings more closely. Actually they are more rebels than kings. Who or what are they?

Perhaps we should begin by asking who is not included. After all, the disturbing thing about the interpretation of Acts 4:27 is that, although the conspiracy includes pagans like Pilate, it also includes Herod. It not only includes the nations of the world but the chosen people. We could say, it includes the church. The revolt against God isn't limited to our "environment." Think how faithless the faithful can be, how pagan the Christian can be, how worldly the church can be. To approach Psalm 2 from Acts 4—to enter the Old Testament from the New Testament—brings with it a needed humility. Actually, we don't need to approach the Old Testament through the New, for already in the Old we only hear about the wicked nations (Ps. 2) *after* we have encountered the wicked among the chosen people (Ps. 1)! Only from this perspective—that is, from church to world—is needed severity to those "outside" appropriate for us.

Apparently the world is still that world of which we read in Genesis 11:4: "Come, let us build ourselves a city, and a tower with its top in the heavens, and let us make a name for ourselves." It's the world of Babel. It's the world that even then made God laugh and mock. We read He actually had to "come down" to reach it—not just because He is so great but because the world is so small. This is the world that is, according to the Bible's beginning, and which is no more, according to the end of the Bible (Rev. 18:1-24). We meet this world not only in its kings but in all those who, in whatever sphere, have something to say or think they have something to say against God. Insolence characterizes the whole gamut of nations, races, and cultures. Who would dare put last in this list the white races and nations, or Western culture?

Nonetheless, the church, which also knows itself judged, may yet pass judgment on all this. This is clearly seen in Revelation 2:26, where we read: "He who conquers and who keeps my works until the end, I will give him power over the nations." And yet, who can conquer and keep God's works to the end? It's that fellow who is strong "like a tree" in Psalm 1. That has something to say to Psalm 2. Why? Because that same man is "like a child."

Ultimate language

What kind of talk is this—of crushing, smashing, dashing to pieces? It's "ultimate language." Van Ruler has said that we must read the Old Testament eschatologically. That is to say, we must not suppose the language we meet in the Psalms is outmoded by our order and civilization and ethic. It also means that we are not to take such language as normative for our own situations, as though we can fling it about in Old Testament manner in all sorts of ways (personally, socially, politically, or militarily). Such language is not out of date but it is reserved for later on. It has a surplus value—not only with reference to its severity but also with reference to its gentleness. Indeed, what is at once so grim and so lovely as the world of the Old Testament? The Psalm is a prophecy of what is to come. It prophesies about the judgment and the grace of which the Messiah is capable.

This doesn't mean we cannot see already here and now something of this judgment. Once the Roman Empire, one of world history's greatest empires, collided with the church. In the end it was the latter which survived and outlived these conflicts and proved stronger. More recently, the German people, one of the most imposing nations and cultures, stalked the Jewish people, the people of Psalm 2, doing away with seven million people. But ultimately its downfall was cataclysmic.

Apostolate

What is the church to do as long as this Psalm with all of its severity is not fulfilled, even though judgment appears about to burst forth? The church doesn't need to learn from the New Testament that before fire can consume Samaria (Luke 9:54), another fire must first burst into flame, the fire of the Holy Spirit (Acts 8:5), or to know that before God's terrifying laughter breaks forth, there is first a laughter from the manger of Bethlehem. The church can learn something of this already in this Psalm—where we read of a kiss before we read about a breaking to pieces and about a going to rack and ruin.

Thank God, we've not yet come to that. We're still in the time of the "kiss." We're still "en route" in the time of reconciliation, the time of the church's mission. The church must understand this mission not only in terms of bringing the gospel to the stone-age culture of New Guinea, but in terms of bringing the gospel where culture is fashioned, where the great decisions of war and peace are made, where great authorities talk about everything and then some.

Whenever rebelliousness appears—and the church is no stranger to such rebelliousness—it will echo the astonished cry of verse 1, "Why, in heaven's name?" Not only because rebellion against the Most High is the most senseless (which it is), but also (and perhaps this amounts to the same thing) because the bonds from which men want to rid themselves are nuptial bonds, cords of love—and the church knows how strong these are! And if these bonds have anything to do with a yoke and a burden—and the church cannot deny this—they have to do with that yoke of which the king in our Psalm says, "my yoke is easy," and with that burden of which he says, "my burden is light" (Matt. 11:30).

MORNING SONG

"I lie down and sleep;
I awake again, for the Lord sustains me."

—Psalm 3:5

We need not doubt that the poet of this Psalm is actually David. Although the superscriptions of the Psalms are not equally reliable, they do have a long tradition behind them. We have no right simply to presuppose that they are necessarily wrong. What we read in this Psalm—"there is no help for him in God"—corresponds strikingly with what we hear Shimei say to David when he was fleeing from Absalom: "The LORD has avenged upon you all the blood of the house of Saul, in whose place you have reigned; and the LORD has given the kingdom into the hand of your son Absalom" (2 Sam. 16:8). Again the mention of the poet's adversaries as "many," later enlarged to include "ten thousands of people," parallels 2 Samuel 15:13, where we read that all Israel took sides with Absalom "from Dan to Beersheba" (2 Sam. 17:11), while the slain soon numbered twenty thousand (2 Sam. 18:7). If indeed the poet of our Psalm is David, he certainly has had a bad time of it.

Bone and marrow

At the outset, let's recognize that he has had an especially hard time of it because of the suggestion that he is forsaken by God—

"there is no help for him in God." What is harder for a believer than that the name of his God should be used against him? This is not only to attack him physically or to break his heart. This is to attack him in that faith on which his life stands or falls.

It must have been especially hard for David to see the "ten thousands of people" not only as ten thousands but as ten thousands of *his* people. His own people are doing this to him. His own son is doing this to him.

Even that isn't the worst of it. His own son has joined the party of the "wicked" to which reference is made. To be sure, we must not take this in too individualistic a manner. We should take it first in objective, and then in subjective, manner. After all, although Psalm 3:7 rejoices in crushing these "wicked," David says to his soldiers, "Deal gently . . . with the young man Absalom" (2 Sam. 18:5). Nor should we take this idea of crushing them too quickly as condemnation. Clearly, however, something has gone through David's bone and marrow (2 Sam. 18:33).

We're acquainted with this

Though he attaches great importance to the authenticity of David's authorship wherever the Psalms make this claim, even J. Ridderbos does not want to read this in merely biographical terms. Instead, he sees it pointing to the vicissitudes of the faithful in every age, past and present.

For that matter, who of us cannot recognize in the "many, many, many" (the word is thrice repeated, not counting the "ten thousands"), if not adversaries, certainly the misfortunes that crowd his own life? Who doesn't realize that these misfortunes, as also for David, become more than misfortunes—that they become temptations? Why should they be only those of which we read in the daily paper—for example, of people in distant Russia? Why not, as also for David, one's own people, one's own party, church, or culture? In short, who doesn't know the "many, many, many" hidden ways in which the word stabs like a dagger, "You will find no help in God"?

A flag is raised

What can one raise against this? What does the poet raise against this? Can we raise anything against it? How far does what "surrounds" us (vs. 6), what we thought we could observe from a distance, touch our own heart? Isn't that the apex of the temptation? How far has our own heart given it occasion? Augustine believed in the existence of the devil, but he also knew that, wherever the devil is, there also are people. He knew this so well that he could say, "The devil is only in our own heart"! Be that as it may, we ought to notice that the poet, when faced with the "many, many, many" who threaten his life in the most existential sense of the word, seems to place little value on what is usually prominent in the Psalms—his own last-ditch stand. Over against the vileness of the temptations he values only God. He seeks his honor only in God. He harnesses Him before the chariot of his own helplessness.

And see! In the midst of the despair of the "many, many, many," and of the sorrows that go through bone and marrow, something triumphant occurs. It's as though a flag is raised (vs. 4). Not that the poet no longer finds himself in a bad spot, or that we no longer find ourselves in a bad spot between those powers that oppress us. But the believer also finds himself between something else, between stronger powers that hold him up and hold him fast. When the poet cries, "For thou dost smite all my enemies on the cheek, thou dost break the teeth of the wicked," what is he doing if not expressing what he knows is true from the power of tradition (yesterday), and what he knows is true in the power of prophecy (tomorrow), and therefore something he knows is true today even if the actuality no longer—or, what is really the same thing, not yet—corresponds to it?

To awake

Accordingly, there's every reason to say "Good night" to one another in the midst of the struggle, and, what is more, to be able to sleep. What is far more: when waking up, not to toss and crawl under the covers again in fear and flight from the day. It means to rise up at length and to say from the bottom of the heart one of the most gloriously cheering things a man can say—"We're still there!" (vs. 5).

We're still there. Why? Not because we deserve to be, but because *He* is still there. He's always there. He'll always be there. In His presence a man doesn't so much wake up as he is awakened by the alarm clock of His power. A man doesn't so much lift up his head as he is lifted up (vs. 3) and brought into the sunlight. It would seem that this happens without our choice—and so it is. We're still there, and we'll always be there because He's always there (Matt. 22:32; Ps. 139). Even after the greatest temptation of all time at Golgotha, even after those three hours of impenetrable darkness, even after the "many, many, many" that pressed in on Him, even after the death that followed—when the greatest temptation for Him was not to show Himself again and so to end His revelation—He arose and was there again and He'll always be there.

Since that time, there is a gracious redundancy in the word of our poet, "Arise, O LORD!" Isn't the "first-born from the dead" (Col. 1:18) always there before us—the most awake of us all in the face of everything that threatens to destroy us? However festive the life of the Jew might be, however many feasts he celebrated, commemorating redemption upon redemption, he did not yet know Easter, the morning feast par excellence. And yet, isn't grace, especially redeeming grace, always something for which one must pray and plead—and for which occasionally one screams?

EVENSONG

Psalm 4 has much in common with Psalm 3. For example, compare verse 6, "There are many who say, 'O that we might see some good!' " with Psalm 3:2, "many are saying of me, there is no help for him in God." For this, as for the reminder of distress and deliverance out of distress (indeed, *in* distress), compare verse 8, "In peace I will both lie down and sleep," with Psalm 3:5, "I lie down and sleep."

Some see the parallels so close that they associate also this Psalm with David's flight from Absalom. In that case, we would need to think of verses 2-5 as addressed to the rebels, especially verse 2: "O men, how long shall my honor suffer shame? How long will you love vain words, and seek after lies?" Others suggest that these words are spoken not to opponents but to partisans who go at it the wrong way and are more hindrance than help. On the basis of verse 4, "Be angry, but sin not," one might argue that this is addressed not to opponents but to questionable friends. That is why J. Ridderbos thinks not of Absalom's followers but of David's followers, people like Joab who caused the king so much grief. It would have to be people *like* Joab, because there is no indication that the king lacked "grain and wine" during the persecution of Absalom. For that reason, Ridderbos places the situation

of Psalm 4 during the time of Saul, before we hear much about
Joab. Be that as it may, the second alternative (the poet's partisans) appears more likely than the first (the poet's opponents).

Pride and doubt

The reference here is not to an opposing party but to a man's
own circle of friends, including some badly off the track. What
track? Trust in God. That's evident in two ways—in the "vain
words" referred to in verse 2, and in the doubt we meet in verse
6. It's evident in pride and in vacillation—and one doesn't exclude the other. The "big men" of verse 2 (for the Hebrew expression indicates men of repute) apparently feel like "whoppers"
one moment and like weasels the next. That's what happens when
a person loses trust in God. His own self-confidence proves to be
both too much and too little.

Clearly, such behavior can be a heavy burden for the good
cause. One might say that militarism on the one hand and defeat-
ism on the other can be more treacherous enemies than the enemy
himself. Job had more trouble with his friends than with his
tempter. Indeed, the latter may have been concealed in the former.

Someone may ask whether the man who talks about the "God
of my righteousness" (K.J.V.) is not himself given to boasting.
Not at all. He doesn't speak of the "God on whom I have a rightful claim." Quite the contrary! After all, the "godly" of verse 3 is
the man who does *not* demand anything of God but simply trusts
in Him. Moreover, as in this instance, doesn't such a confession
of faith in one way or another often lead to suffering? It's a hum-
bling experience.

God and the good

In what does such trust in God consist? For one thing, when
the "many" say, "Who will shew us any good?" (K.J.V.)—which
may include all sorts of good in the midst of all sorts of want, including a literal lack of "grain and wine"—we will not join them,

especially when these "many" try to save themselves from this
want, no matter what means they employ (verse 2). We will not
do this, even though we have questions of our own. For that matter, the poet doesn't wear his heart on his sleeve. Not that we let
everything happen to us without making vigorous response. The
poet takes it as self-evident that there is a place for anger—just so
long as one does not sin. The latter is the case when in all sorts
of questions we've lost the answer—that is to say, when in the absence of various goods we forget the presence of *the* good. It happens when we forget what Christ later will express in the words
"No one is good but God alone" (Mark 10:18). The believer is
recognized as one who, when the chips are down, will try to identify the good with God, instead of trying to identify God with the
good. Can we find the good ultimately apart from God? Only He
can take care of the good because, when all is said and done, only
He is the good. We can be glad, of course, when His presence
and when the presence of "grain and wine" do not pose a dilemma.
But if this be the case, the choice should not be too difficult.
We are better off with Him alone than with "grain and wine"
alone (Ps. 84:10). Not that the one—or rather, the One—isn't
linked with the other, or that God will not bring along all other
good with Himself. We can even say that the relation between
God and the good comes out more clearly in the Old Testament
than in the New, although in the latter also we read that, if we
seek first the Kingdom of God, all other things will be added—
clothing, food, and drink (Matt. 6:33). That is to say, when we
think of the good we're not forbidden to think of all sorts of material, earthly, and temporal joys. The prophets can portray a ver-
itable paradise! But this may take awhile. In the definitive sense
of the word, we'll have to wait until the New Jerusalem for this
paradise. In the meantime, we lose sight at times of the relation
between God and the good because it isn't always easy to see it.
But that's no reason for us, when we find ourselves left in the
lurch by the good, to try to grab for it like the men of verse 2, or
to despair about it like the fearful in verse 6. God's presence
ought to keep us from impudence and from despair.

The song

We can go even further. With the poet of Psalm 3 or with the poet of Psalm 4, there's every reason to come to a true rest in the evening of the wearily fought day or year or life—provided we know how to answer the challenge posed in this Psalm. It's the challenge that the prophet Habakkuk knew how to answer when he said:

> Though the fig tree do not blossom,
>   nor fruit be on the vines,
> the produce of the olive fail
>   and the fields yield no food,
> the flock be cut off from the fold
>   and there be no herd in the stalls,
> yet I will rejoice in the LORD . . .

These are impressive verses. Habakkuk's sighing begins with a prayer and ends with a song, a song with "stringed instruments," if you please (Habakkuk 3:1-19)! The challenge is whether we have such trust in God that, when we must stand before God alone, this trust will be more than an abstraction. And what is less abstract than a song? Whether we sing that song, or mutter it, or even moan it at the evening of a day, a year, or a lifetime, the lack of everything and anything is reckoned and weighed (Ps. 90:10), but also the cover of trust in God is offered us, and a mighty Hand is placed on our forehead.

This is what the Psalmist offers those who have tried seeking this by themselves and, in so doing, have come either to pride or to faintheartedness, so that they meditate on it silently (vs. 4) before managing a song, as he did in his Psalm. Perhaps they won't quite manage to bring it to a song, because they are ashamed. But, might someone else not be able to manage a song about *them*? That would not be so altogether different. It might even be better instead of worse!

OUTLOOK

> "... *in the morning I prepare a sacrifice for thee, and watch.*"
>
> —Psalm 5:3

Although this Psalm, like Psalm 3, is a morning song—perhaps because it is a morning song—the (Dutch) superscription calls it a morning *prayer*. A believer too can have "morning sickness"! The Psalm is uttered with more sighing—is born of more sighing —than is Psalm 3. The poet must have misgivings about something. Well then, what better can he do than to incorporate his mood into a prayer? Luther used to do this. When he had misgivings about a particular day, especially when he was very busy, when he had a host of anxieties and when a host of fears and devils surrounded him like "tiles on the roof," Luther would begin the day with a long prayer that took a lot of time. We might think this a strange logic because he really didn't have time for it. Perhaps we would do well not only to be surprised but to learn something from it.

God's righteousness

Evidently, the poet, whoever he may be, doesn't expect anything from his own strength, action, or righteousness.

Our first impression might be different. On the one hand, he sees people of whom he can say, "For there is no truth in *their* mouth." On the other hand, he says of himself, "But *I* . . ." That doesn't appeal to us. Our false modesty finds it a bit suspect. When we hear him say, "For thou dost bless the righteous, O LORD," we're apt to regard this as arbitrary and presumptuous. But that's wrong—if for no other reason than that the poet directs himself to God in prayer at a time when the morning sacrifice is being brought into the temple. Today we might say that he brings this prayer as his morning sacrifice. That's hardly self-righteousness or lack of surrender. To be sure, we know well enough that Pharisees are able to make even out of prayer a demonstration of pride (Luke 18:11: "God, I thank thee that I am not like other men"!), but in that kind of thanksgiving prayer as petition disappears altogether.

Again, notice his terminology. What he is and what he does, he is and does "through the abundance of thy steadfast love." He can't do it without direction. "Lead me, O LORD, in thy righteousness." That strikes the same note as "lead us not into temptation." Indeed, it's really the same thing. Think also of such expressions as "bowing down" ("worship"), and "in the fear of thee." The poet isn't fretting about some way in which he can find shelter by himself. He only wants to find "shelter with thee." And, when he comes to joy and confidence in living, it's because he knows "thou dost cover."

Social righteousness

It would be possible for all this to go to his head and make him a Pharisee were it not for the fact that he doesn't utter any of this for his own private enjoyment. What he says doesn't go to his head; instead, it reaches out to his neighbor and brings him to his neighbor. He not only addresses himself *to* God but also *against* "those who speak lies," against the "bloodthirsty and deceitful men," against people who "flatter with their tongue" but—watch out—whose "throat is an open sepulchre." In other words, he's against flatterers who are evildoers.

The temple, where the poet bows in fear of the Lord, stands for the opposite of all this. It stands for speaking the truth and for making common life possible. It stands for trustworthiness, for the fact that people can approach each other. What is this temple today, what must it be, if not the church?

Ultimate righteousness

His indignation against what those who speak lies do and allow, against these bloodthirsty and deceitful men, is so extreme that the poet cries out: "Make them bear their guilt, O God; let them fall by their own counsels; because of their many transgressions cast them out, for they have rebelled against thee."

We must not be embarrassed too quickly by this on the basis of the New Testament. As though the New Testament had only a climate of forgiveness and not also one of indignation! Always we have to watch out not to fall below the norm of biblical gentleness *and* of biblical severity. Believers can rejoice that one day it will be all over for the regime of liars, of bloodthirsty and deceitful men, of faithless men on earth.

Of course, this will be joy only for those believers who understand faith as more than believing and who themselves have come to deeds of truth and love. There's no excuse for anyone who misses this—being a blessing for his neighbor—also to skip over what's been said about being a curse for the constant deceivers (verse 10 speaks of "many transgressions") of his neighbor. If we lack the former, we may not take refuge in the latter. That would indeed be a *false* modesty! Because of the latter's necessity we have to come to the former. That's the way things are—so severe and so gentle.

Outlook

We come to what we have entitled "outlook." It ought to be evident that this doesn't have anything to do with sitting "poetically" in front of the window and lifting up our heart to the morning air. Of course we can enjoy the morning air, but what a pity if we were content with that. That's what the poet Rilke did—he said that the sense of sin was alien to him because he experienced "such pure mornings." It's obvious that the things mentioned have nothing to do with the poet's opposite. That would be the drudge who thinks he has to fix everything himself and for that reason gets up so early. Of such a man the Bible says in Psalm 127:2, "It is vain that you rise up early."

But all this has little if anything to do with the outlook we meet here. To summarize what we have said, we note three things. First, this Psalm offers us an outlook on God's righteousness. Second, it offers an outlook on social righteousness. Third, it offers an outlook on the end of all unrighteousness. For "death shall be no more, neither shall there be mourning nor crying nor pain any more" (Rev. 21:4). If, in the first instance, our Psalm is a sighing Psalm, more a prayer than a song, in the end there is jubilation (vs. 12)!

LOVE OF LIFE

". . . in Sheol who can give thee praise?"

—Psalm 6:5

Two things arrest our attention in this Psalm—what the poet does and what he says. First, what he does.

What the poet does

With unusual frankness he proceeds to tell God exactly what is on his heart. He may have ended with something else, but he certainly did not begin with that. With what? With saying, "Thy will be done." First he wants to tell his God very specifically what is *his* will. One could even say that he hasn't wanted to leave God free to make His decision. It seems as though he uses his prayer primarily to inform God about his own decision.

In a way, we're reminded of that unusual counsel the people praying in Jerusalem received from Isaiah. We read: "You who put the LORD in remembrance, take no rest." There's nothing unusual about that. But notice what follows: "and give *him* no rest" (Isa. 62: 6-7). Let's not suppose that only in a few instances in the Bible does God see Himself pressured by men's prayers. The whole Bible, and the Psalter in particular, teems with such situations from which we might shrink on the supposition that we give the Lord more pleasure by letting Him rest as much as possible, by not bothering Him. But wrongly so.

Could that be the reason we are troubled so often by something of which the poet doesn't have to complain—namely, that his prayer remains unanswered? We recall the familiar story of King Hezekiah who also prayed earnestly and who was heard wondrously (Isa. 38:1-22).

In view of that story, and in view of the no less sudden reversal in verses 8 and 9 of our Psalm, who has the right to make generalizations in random fashion about the immutability of God? It is possible to speak of this in defensible manner, but not in random generalizations. That might make for a very philosophical but not a very merciful God! As God is almighty in His love, so He is immutable in His *love*. To speak of love is to speak of movement, of variation, of changeableness. In this sense we could say that our God is unchangeably changeable, *always love*. ". . . gracious and merciful, slow to anger, and abounding in steadfast love, and repents of evil" (Joel 2:13). Let no one say this is only a very human way of talking about God. Would it were typically human! No, this is a divine way of talking about God. God's repentance means everything to Him.

What the poet says

Apart from what he does, the second thing we notice is what the poet *says*: ". . . in Sheol who can give thee praise?"

He sees death as punishment. If we were to tell him what the Heidelberg Catechism says—that death "is a passage to eternal life" and that therefore he ought to look at death more cheerfully —he would reply that if death is also this, well and good, but that he still sees death as punishment. The same would be true of his praying. He would say that if a person can still pray "Thy will be done," well and good, but for him there's no reason to begin this way!

The poet doesn't mean that in death God will no longer think of us. In this respect the mood of the Psalms is not pessimistic. Each of us knows to his comfort Psalm 139:8: "If I make my bed in Sheol, thou art there!" No, he doesn't mean that in death

God will no longer think of him—even though, to be honest, it's not easy to conceive of this. Instead, he wants to say that we can't think of God when we're dead. To be sure, one might contrast this with a typical New Testament "knowledge"—such as the picture of the souls "under the altar" who beseech the Almighty for righteousness to come at last (Rev. 6:9-10). Still, those under the altar are no longer—or not yet—fully human for they are no longer—or not yet—there bodily. In fact, they literally have no mouth to praise God. However we may conceive of the praise of God by those who have fallen asleep, suspended between the day of their death and the last day, at best it would seem to be "half work." It remains true: ". . . in Sheol who can give thee praise?" Not simply because *I* can't come into my own very well. That's true enough. We humans don't feel quite at home with the angels. We only feel at home when we have both feet on the ground. But it's also true because *God* can't fully come into His own with all such "half" people who can't get along without their bodies to praise Him adequately.

This is not to say that God only needs our *mouth* to be praised. Read again how sorrow over his approaching death consumed Hezekiah. When he thinks of what the praise of God includes, he thinks not only of all we may say or sing to God, but of this whole precious life on earth that makes life worth living—all the years, all the people around me, all that life from which I cannot separate myself. Don't we want to praise God with all of this?

Jesus and Hezekiah

". . . in Sheol who can give thee praise?" Some time ago I read a meditation on this text—I think it appeared in the weekly *In de waagschaal.* The writer was objecting to those who, reading words like this, are apt to say, "How typically Old Testament! How impoverished! The man doesn't know any better!" He rejected this attitude by appealing to the event of Easter morning when Jesus broke the bonds of death and in principle brought to an end the realm of death. What else did Jesus do, according to the writer, but what the writer of this Psalm and what Hezekiah did, by saying: "Indeed, in Sheol there is no praise of God and that's why I'm making an end of it!" I think he was quite right.

The guards became as dead men

To remember our Savior is to remember something else— namely, that death is not only punishment but judgment. Perhaps we should say that death is not only suffering but guilt. Death is more than biological death. For that matter, has death ever been only biological death for anyone? The valley of the shadow of death, in which the poet finds himself, is at the same time the battlefield of God's wrath.

Nevertheless, even without pointing to the Savior, the poet already knows that something else can be said about death and is being said about it. He cries: "Depart from me, all you workers of evil; for the Lord has heard the sound of my weeping. The Lord has heard my supplication; the Lord accepts my prayer. All my enemies shall be ashamed and sorely troubled; they shall turn back, and be put to shame in a moment."

What a splendid Easter text! Think of the guards at the tomb —they "became like dead men" (Matt. 28:4)!

Actually, who are the poet's enemies? Now we know who they are. Whoever they may have been, they are those who want me *dead,* whereas God wants me alive. Certainly they are those who don't believe a word of what we've been saying. Unbelief lacks the true love of life.

NO WHINING

*". . . judge me, O Lord, according to my righteousness
and according to the integrity that is in me."*

—Psalm 7:8

Again we hear the same note as in Psalm 1, and again our first
reaction is negative. Again we're struck with our greatest fright,
our fear of pharisaism. Who of us dares to say offhand about
himself what the poet says? Who of us dares to point God to his
own righteousness and integrity? The whole of the gospel, and especially Jesus Christ, seems to forbid our doing this. And not only
the world of the gospel. In the Psalms also another note is struck.
Listen, for example, to Psalm 14:2-3: "The LORD looks down
from heaven upon the children of men, to see if there are any that
act wisely, that seek after God. They have all gone astray, they
are all alike corrupt; there is none that does good, no, not one."
Nor is this an exception. We recall Psalm 51:5: "I was brought
forth in iniquity, and in sin did my mother conceive me."

No whining

The last note, however, makes it clear that we cannot speak of
sin everywhere and always in the same way—but only of sin in
the "then and there" (e.g., David and Bathsheba!). Just because
I'm a sinner and will always be a sinner doesn't mean that I do
nothing but sinful stunts! Once our little boy didn't want to say
his prayers before going to bed. When I asked why, he replied

that he hadn't committed any sins that day. That may be an exaggeration (in his case it was!), but I'd rather hear this than a man who loves nothing better than to talk about his sins so much that he wallows in them. (That happens more often and seems much worse to me.) Just because we may always have wars and rumors of wars doesn't mean that we have to regard war as inevitable—and it certainly must not deter us from seeing to it that the number of conflicts be kept as few as possible. That was the greatness of Hammarskjöld, the late-lamented secretary-general of the United Nations. He knew the art of stamping out as many fires as possible without any illusions about the power or presence of fire. Christians must know situations in whose tragedy they have neither part nor lot, for which very reason they are able to do something about these situations.

The Bible doesn't share our whining about sin or our sickly fear of pharisaism. To be sure, the note we heard in Psalm 14 is there, and it is terribly true. But so is the note struck in our Psalm there, and, thank God, it can be no less true. It's so true that the whole judgment of the world is included in it.

Not "offhand"

A little while ago we said, "Who would dare say this in offhand manner about himself?" In our Psalm it's not said in offhand manner. It's not just a cry, it's demonstrated! The poet says: "If I have rewarded evil unto him that was at peace with me; (yea, I have delivered him that without cause is mine enemy:) . . ." (K.J.V.). We recall the story of David. Pursued by Saul as by a murderer, David did not seize his opportunity to pay Saul back for all the misery he himself had endured, and attain at last a peaceable and even royal life. Instead, he "spared a man who wronged me"—and he did this twice (1 Sam. 24:7; 26:9)!

Nota bene

Fear of pharisaism must not keep a Christian from being a decent person—and a lot more! Recall what Jesus said about this.

He never made light of the righteousness of the Pharisees. On the contrary, he commanded his disciples to seek a righteousness that exceeded theirs (Matt. 5:10). Again, recall such words as these: "For if you love those who love you, what reward have you?" Again: "And if you salute only your brethren, what more are you doing than others? Do not even the Gentiles do the same?" (Matt. 5:46, 47).

Let no one suppose that anything unusual is here being asked him. That might be true for people in general but not for a Christian! In this Psalm the question cannot be raised as we often like to put it: Is this permissible? Isn't this pharisaical? There is only one legitimate response: This has to be so; this is Christian.

Only so will our righteousness begin to correspond a bit with God's righteousness. He has always done more than He had to. He has always requited evil with good while sparing His enemies. He has always done so and, through the appearing of Jesus Christ, He has done it in particular. That's why we may expect more from the people of the New Testament than from those of the Old. A little scoop is added—a scoop of love. But how does the Christian respond to the Old Testament man when the latter wears himself out in love? Nota bene. He asks whether this isn't pharisaism!

Conversion

If we're not like our poet, there's only one thing left for us— conversion. Else we've had it.

Someone may suggest that in the world of the Psalms only the wicked have had it. Indeed. In the Psalms, however, the wicked are the unconverted—those unconverted in their relationship to God are those unconverted in their relationship to the neighbor. If that's true of the world of the Psalms, let's hope it's not different in the church, in our church. The wicked are people who turn their backs on God and their neighbor.

Of course there are people who readily admit that they are in wrong relationship to God and neighbor. They love nothing more than to admit this. They're always doing it—until it makes you sick. They acknowledge that everything is wrong but, alas, there's not much that can be done about it because . . . There they go again. We're sinners and will always be sinners. They even think this perpetual confession of weakness is quite courageous—at least very pious—because it's very humble and certainly not pharisaical. I think the Psalm would count such folk among the wicked. After all, isn't it obvious that they believe in their own wickedness more than in God's saving righteousness?

Because they're so afraid of pharisaism, they're more concerned about their own wickedness than about God's righteousness. Fear of pharisaism is very convenient—in fact, sinfully convenient. It throws us into fits and poisons the church with everything in and around it.

Pray and work

In the world of the gospel it's the same as in that of the Psalms. When the Lord Jesus teaches us to pray, he teaches us two things, and he teaches us to pray one right after the other: ". . . forgive us our debts" and "as we forgive out debtors" (Matt. 6:12, K.J.V.).

Only if we pray these two together can we be sure that we'll be heard in what follows: "And lead us not into temptation" (Matt. 6:13). ". . . forgive us our debts" will keep us from pharisaism. ". . . as we forgive our debtors" will keep us from being so stuck in fear of pharisaism that we are unable to move toward God and neighbor. One could also call that a false modesty. In point of fact, however, we'd better pray for this. Happily, prayers are meant to be heard, especially if, like the poet, we don't leave it with praying but also work for it. This combination of praying and working will keep us from not ever trying to do anything or, like a Pharisee, from being too sure of what we do.

THE CHILD AND THE KING

". . . little less than divine . . ."

—Psalm 8:5 (Moffatt)

Man is the crown of creation, as the superscription of our Psalm reads in the New (Dutch) translation. That's quite something! Evidently this doesn't simply refer to man as he was, man in some fancied long ago, man in paradise—despite the past tense of verse 5. No, it refers to man as he is, fallen man—for verse 6 is again in the present tense. In spite of everything, man is the crown of creation. What an astonishing story! Nor can we doubt this when we look around us. Never has there been such a colossal development of civilization as in the mastery of nature today. That's what Psalm 8 is all about. Consider the word "all" which we meet in the verse "thou hast put all things under his feet." It's beginning to look like it! The great heavens, the work of God's fingers, the "the moon and the stars which thou hast established," this whole tremendous environment of little man—he can actually reach it all. Men have been to the moon and who knows how much farther they will go! It's no exaggeration to say that in our day Pslam 8 is being fulfilled a little. A little—for who knows what may not be embraced in that enigmatic phrase "little less than divine"? According to biologists, man is hardly different from the animals—and yet, a "little less than God"! Whatever it means, it's hard to be surprised by anything that may lie ahead in the future. Our most audacious dreams may yet be realized.

Demythologizing

No one can doubt this and no one should be afraid of it, as though this whole adventure is forbidden to Christians. Some Christians may suppose such audacity is out of place, but they have the Bible against them. Psalm 8 contradicts them far more than it supports them. Indeed, we must express this more strongly. After all, why should an eerie awe of limitless space and of man's mastery of nature keep some Christians from sharing in the great discoveries of our time instead of being enthusiastic about it all? Wasn't it rather the pagan who had such terrifying awe of what we call "nature"—supposing nature to be divine, or a part of God, or even God Himself? A man who imagines the moon to be some kind of goddess is not likely to try a trip to the moon— not even in his most audacious dreams! Of course we have no right to say that genuine development of culture is possible only in Christian lands. The achievements of Cain's line suggest otherwise (Gen. 4:20-21). But we do have to admit that wherever believers have moved into the realm of nature the latter has been effectively demythologized and prepared for what we call the modern age. Jew and Christian have always had less scruples than the pagans about laying open the creation—and rightly so. The first commandment did not forbid this—indeed, it commanded this. The theme of Psalm 8 is that of the creation story of Genesis, challenging the reader to subdue the earth (Gen. 1:28). "Go ahead," God says, "it's yours."

Public and particular

This has far-reaching implications. For example, it may not be sufficiently self-evident to some of us that the public (state) universities have a place as well as the private (Christian) universities.[1] I mention universities because these are especially

---

1. TRANSLATOR'S NOTE: While we also have our public and private (including church-related colleges and universities) the author is thinking especially of the place which the Free University in Amsterdam has had for his denomination (The Reformed Churches of the Netherlands), contrasted with the place the state universities have in the Netherlands Reformed Church.

engaged in the terrain described in Psalm 8. God has made these public institutions also a "little less than divine." To them also He gives "dominion over the works of [his] hands." Christians who don't happen to study in a "Christian" university shouldn't feel threatened. The summons and the blessing of Psalm 8 hold true for them and for their university. The Psalm doesn't say that the Christian but that man is the crown of creation. However marred the image of God may be in man's relation to God, however ravaged in its relation to his neighbor, these consequences are seen least in man's relation to nature. That's why Kuyper,[2] in his great work, *Common Grace,* could use such bold language. That study is really a great exegesis of Psalm 8.

As children

Man is quite a man over against the animal world and matter. From these he knows how to deliver himself. But over against God? Man doesn't seem to need God. That's why this same man needs to learn something about the size of "babes and infants," as we read in verse 2.

We know what that means. Anyone who has seen a small infant or child snatching for air knows what it means. The image suggests utter dependence. We recall what Jesus said about it (Matt. 18:3). He might say today, "Unless you become like children, you may reach the moon, but not the kingdom of God."

We are not children anymore. We have self-consciousness. We know who we are. Nonetheless, what else is the realization of dependence if not thanksgiving and wonder? And the wonder is this: how did almighty God ever get it into His head to make me, a little "whippersnapper" under the stars, the crown of creation? Who would ever have gotten it into his head to suggest or think this? Consequently, all we do know is that we must offer praise not to ourselves or to man in general, but to God. That is why, al-

---

2. TRANSLATOR'S NOTE: Abraham Kuyper (d. 1920) led the secession resulting in the formation of the Gereformeerde Kerken. He made a lasting impress on primary and secondary education, politics, and theology. He founded the Free University, and was briefly prime minister of the Netherlands. Of his many theological works, *Common Grace,* is the most significant.

though the middle of the Psalm praises man, its beginning and end sing the praise of God. The latter embraces the former.

To offer such praise we have to go from the realm of culture to the church. If the former is characterized by "man," the latter is characterized by "child." If the former summons us to work, the latter summons us to worship. If the rest of the week symbolizes the realm of culture, Sunday symbolizes the life of the church.

The Lamb and the harvest

That man is great and almost divine is not wrong. It would be wrong were this not so and were he not sharing in the great discoveries of our time. Then he wouldn't be able to enter into the world of Psalm 8. Then the Lord God might well prefer the betas to the alphas. What is wrong is when man ceases to be astonished that he is so amazingly great, so little less than divine. There's the real enemy of verse 2. It's the person who no longer recognizes the church as well as culture, worship as well as work, for whom Sunday has disappeared in the week, and for whom the child is lost in the man.

All this not only is "not good"; it's "not very secure." In the long run, such a man will go to pieces with his culture. Or, even though his civilization and culture may come on the new earth, he will not save himself by it. He will be left in the lurch. That's the way in which mighty Babylon falls to the new Jerusalem. That's why it's the Lamb and not the world of culture who gains the harvest at the end of history.

The Son of David

However, the one doesn't exclude but includes the other. We have a perfect example in David, the author of many Psalms. Who could be both so childlike and so mighty as this king? Or take his people, the Jewish people. What people has been so continually humbled by suffering while achieving so much in the world of culture? Even so, we haven't yet come to the example of greatest dependence and of greatest authority ever expressed on earth—Jesus Christ.

Who prayed with such childlike dependence and obedience as He prayed in Gethsemane? Who ruled the creation as He who, when still an infant, drew the stars to Himself (Matt. 2:9), who was "with the wild beasts" (Mark 1:13), who could still storms, overthrow death, and undertake an actual ascension? No wonder that the writer of the Letter to the Hebrews applied Psalm 8 particularly to Him (Heb. 2:5-8).

The Son of man

This is not to suggest that the portrait no longer applies to us. On the contrary, it applies *properly* to us, for all this is prophetic. If, as the writer of Hebrews says, we do not yet *see* all things put under man's feet (and, indeed, we don't), then, as he goes on to say, we must look to Jesus (Heb. 2:9). In Him we see it already. In Him we hope one day to walk on waves, to still storms, to undertake ascensions, and to break down walls. A man can hope for that!

And not only he! The whole creation is eagerly longing—as a hungry sparrow—"for the revealing of the sons of God" (Rom. 8:19). A time will come when our hands will not longer be set against God's creation but able to clasp all that's in it. That day is the last day, the day of absolute dependence and absolute praise.

En route

Perhaps then work will include worship, culture the church, the week Sunday, and man the Christian, so that the latter is wholly taken up in the former. Perhaps, as earlier I expressed appreciation for public life, a word of appreciation is in order now for the special Christian activities in which we're engaged "en route." In this light these often-abused activities are unbelievably promising.

MORTALS

> *"Arise, O Lord, let not mortal man prevail,*
> *let the nations be judged in Thy sight.*
> *Put them in fear, O Lord,*
> *that the nations may know they are mortal."*
>
> —Psalm 9:19-20 (Dutch rendering)

Literally, the Hebrew reads "man" rather than "mortal." The latter translation of the Netherland Bible Society can pose a difficult question for us. Is being human the same as being mortal? It makes us ask whether death was present "from the beginning." Even if death may not belong to the "last" things which still remain but which happily at last have "passed away" (as Rev. 21:4 says), would it not still belong to the "first" things? Is death natural? We're not thinking here of *our* death, for this is called the wages of sin (Rom. 6:23). We're thinking here of biological death as over against theological death (if you'll pardon this unhappy expression). Using the language of paradise, it would make a difference to say that Adam would have died anyhow—even if differently. Apparently that's what we have to say about animals. Long before man's appearance in history are traces of animal existence that bear witness to death, even to prodigious death. Already Luther, who of course knew nothing about evolution, thought he had to suppose this, though he made an exception for man. He thought man could have won immortality. There's still disagreement about this question.

Mere creature

It's hard to improve on the translation "mortal" because, actually, the reader has no choice. However it might have been, to be human now means to be mortal. To be exact, in Hebrew the expression doesn't precisely mean "being human." A connotation is hidden in it that makes us think of humanness in its weakest rather than in its strongest sense. That's another reason why it's hard to improve on the translation "mortal." We may think of the concept "flesh," which always has a weak rather than a strong connotation. We think of "fragile," "transient," "perishable." Most English translations render it "but man" (= only man). This seems a bit demeaning to me. I prefer the rendering in an English commentary in which the "but" is replaced by "mere." I think the expression "mere creature" does more justice than the expression "only men" except that it offers us more opportunity to interpret this in sympathetic "paradisical" manner as well as in antipathetic "fallen" manner.

Perhaps the best way of dealing with the initial question and with the most precise rendering is simply to say that man is that creature who cannot sustain life for himself. That's not the sad thing about him, and certainly not the sinful thing. The sad thing is that he wanted to try it and that he still tries it. And that's also the sinful thing about him. In doing this, his humanness, his mortality, and his sinfulness become synonymous.

A prayer

". . . let not mortal man prevail" becomes a prayer: "Lord God Almighty, let not man try to make it on his own on the earth. He's a creature who can't even keep himself alive. He can't make it on his own now because, look, he dies—how he dies! He never could make it on his own because, when he tried it, he died a thousand deaths (Gen. 3:3, 19). For that matter, he can't keep anything alive if You let him have his own way—whether it be his marriage, his children, his songs, his knowledge. If You don't

take care of him, Lord God Almighty, he'll kill everything today
or tomorrow in a bitter atomic death. You know this, for he
didn't spare You on Golgotha. His own catechism tells him that
he's even able to kill the One who is most alive, God. Nietzsche is
right. No, let not man prevail!"

A curse

But this isn't all that's prayed for in the Psalm. There's something more: "Put them in fear, O LORD!"

The answer to this prayer isn't simply an Old Testament affair
but still occurs from time to time—with a vengeance. It occurs in
such fashion that we all think of the lines "Thou hast rebuked
the nations, thou hast destroyed the wicked; thou hast blotted out
their name for ever and ever. The enemy have vanished in everlasting ruins; their cities thou hast rooted out; the very memory of
them has perished" (vss. 5-6). Our thoughts go back to Berlin in
1945, when an enemy of God's people crumbled as seldom an enemy of that people has crumbled—so much so that it seemed an
eternity would elapse before the German people could again receive a name among the nations. However, in such descriptions
and for such fulfillment on the last day, we do well to think not
only of nations but of men—and not always of other nations and
of other men. The application of the concept "wicked" in the
Psalms, as Ridderbos has shown, is not necessarily reserved for
others. The poet has his own wickedness. He knows it and con-
fesses it.

A blessing

That God puts men and nations in fear so that they may realize
to the full their mortality is not an outdated idea. Happily, there's
something else that is not out of date. When the Christian hears
the Jew call on our God to rise up, he thinks not only in general
terms but in particular of Golgotha and of the terror awakened
there. Then, too, men were made aware of their nothingness, for
the guards "became like dead men" (Matt. 28:4).

At the same time, we are aware more than ever before how savingly this fear is intended. Before fear struck those guards, graves spring open. We could even say that men spring out of mortality and sinfulness (Matt. 27:52-53). What happened then anticipates the time when death will be no more, "neither shall there be mourning nor crying nor pain any more," the time of an unexpected but always hoped for immortality (Rev. 21:4). What the children of Adam couldn't manage on their own is simply given to the children of God (Luther)!

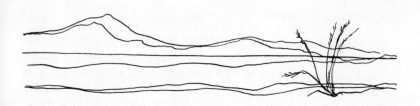

THE JUGGLER'S HAND

"Thou dost see; yea, thou dost note trouble and vexation, that thou mayest take it into thy hands . . ."

—Psalm 10:14

The poet's life is embittered by the wicked. These could be domestic as well as foreign foes, though something can be said for the view that Psalm 9 refers more to the latter while Psalm 10 refers more to the former. There are wicked deeds foreigners can do to a man, and there are wicked deeds done to a man from within his own circle when believers behave badly toward one another. There are wicked deeds within as well as without the church. And there are wicked deeds a man can do to himself. The Psalms are acquainted with this also. To summarize, life in its totality can make a very wicked impression. "The years of our life are threescore and ten, or even by reason of strength fourscore; yet their span is but toil and trouble" (Ps. 90:10). Indeed, an ungodly amount of toil and trouble!

Appearance and reality

Ungodly? Most of all when God seems to stay away from it, when, as the poet says at the outset of our Psalm, God is absent. The Psalm begins by putting a question mark after the very God who can still be called an exclamation point par excellence! The Psalm begins with "Why?" Nor is this the only Psalm that begins

with or is acquainted with this question. Many which may not use
the word "why" literally are no less acquainted with the
question. Not only many Psalms but many Christians as well have
the impression that an ungodly amount of toil and trouble has
pushed even the thought of God clear out of their lives.

That's the impression they have. That's the way it seems—reality is quite otherwise. That's why the Psalmist returns to his question—because he can't seem to let go of it. Of course, faith has
appearance against it. Life certainly seems to be an ungodly
business when one looks at people who cause an ungodly
amount of toil and trouble, or at people who have to endure an
ungodly amount of toil and trouble. Indeed, faith has appearance
against it, but reality for it. That's something else again.

The detective of suffering

We must examine this more closely. What's done about all this
toil and trouble that overtake me? First of all—and that's already
enormously significant—it is recognized. The Bible doesn't cir-
cumvent my lot, isn't silent about it, and doesn't speak of it casually. The Bible doesn't make my toil and trouble less than it is.
Indeed, only when I've read the Bible do I realize how serious
things are! The Bible doesn't make a random guess about it. If
there's one book in which I can feel myself completely understood
and taken seriously in this respect (as in every respect), it's the
Bible. That's the first thing.

The second is that all this is seen in a particular way. We read:
"Thou dost *see*." "See" is too tame a word for a much more serious affair. It might tempt us to conclude that God is good enough
to glance at my toiling once in awhile, but then turns away to de-
vote Himself again to His own strictly divine activities. Not so. In
Hebrew, the little word "see" means to concentrate on seeing
something, to study it. God studies the toil and trouble of people
and what life does to them. We could say that He spies on the
things mentioned, that He wants to be a detective, that He's at it
day and night.

He can't leave it alone

Because of the way in which the Psalm begins, someone might still say, He sees it "afar off." Such a person might say, "All right, God looks at it. He has an excellent spyglass. But He himself may still be far away." Once again, this is appearance rather than reality. Actually, we've answered this already by saying that He studies it. It's answered even more by what follows. We read that He sees it all so that He may take it into His hands. Here two readings are possible. One can take this as the close of the former verse, as is done in the new (Dutch) translation. One can also take this as the beginning of a new sentence. Then it would read, "In order to leave it in thy hands, the hapless commits himself to thee." That reading is a little weaker. Then God wouldn't Himself take it into His hands, but another would do that. The latter reading is less likely. Actually, however, it comes down to the same thing. It comes to this—God can't leave my trouble alone, either with His eyes or with His hands. If the one (eyes) would still allow us to say "afar off," the other (hands) will not allow this. If you want to pick something up, you have to come very close to it, don't you?

The heavenly official

Now comes the real question, that which really matters. God may be aware of my toil and trouble and He may indeed have picked it up—but then what? An official can do that too, in very friendly manner, while sitting in his chair. He can pick up the dossier of my case and say, "You have my attention—my special attention—for yours is an emergency case, a very urgent matter." Yet even so, I might not hear any more about it. Sometimes the Lord God seems to be like a big official—no doubt the friendliest of all—a heavenly official in His heavenly chair, who takes up my toil and trouble and says He will give me his special attention. But then?

The image doesn't fit. It may constitute a temptation for us and especially for the Jew. But anyone who has been to Golgotha knows better. There the image is not of someone sitting in a chair, but of someone hanging on a cross—and that's not like an official at all. Nor does He simply take something in His hand. No, He gets something through His hand—a nail. We know all this well enough. What is this nail if not my toil and trouble? And then?

Then something happens! Then what we find in Psalm 9 is confirmed: "For the needy shall not always be forgotten, and the hope of the poor shall not perish for ever."

Then He rises from the dead! Then something *happens*. At last, something happens! We've always waited for this!

The juggler's hand

To be sure, life is toil and trouble—whether we're seventy or, if we're strong, eighty years of age (Ps. 90:10). And it may take longer. When Christ sums it up in Matthew 24, it almost seems as though there will be no end of it, for the most terrible thing we read there is that "the end is not yet."

Still, it's not endless. At the end a tree arises. There is a horizon, green and fruitful (vss. 32-33). Even that isn't the greatest wonder. The greatest wonder is not that after all the misery a tree puts forth its leaves in Matthew 24, or that after all the water there is wine at Cana, or that at Golgotha there is a resurrection after the grave. Rather, the wonder is that out of (indeed, in) all the misery something grows—that wine appears out of (indeed, in) that water, that out of (indeed, in) that grave something rises.

And so, in our text, the great Juggler of all takes our toil and trouble into His great hand. Whether we're seventy or even eighty years of age, we watch in breathless wonder. And, lo, a rabbit of supreme joy springs into view and hops away over the new earth.

The evil hunter

I suppose someone may think this a poor joke or an image too good to be true. He'll think of another image drawn from another little rhyme that seems more true. It's a little verse all of us in Holland know, the one about the green-green-green-green-turnip-

turnip-turnip-field. There too something comes hopping along—not a rabbit but a hare. No matter. But then comes the evil hunter, and the story is ended. That's the way life seems.

However, the poet and the church say that no matter how often this may be so, one day it will no longer be so. One day *this* will be over! The poet and the church believe—I refer to the last verse of the Psalm—that a day will come when "man who is of the earth may strike terror no more." That is to say, one day not one evil hunter will appear any more to shoot down the joy.

CONCERNING VIOLENCE

". . . and his soul hates him that loves violence."

—Psalm 11:5

In Psalm 11, as in Psalm 1, we meet the antithesis of the righteous and the wicked. We've already seen that in the world of the Psalms the wicked is the man who is indifferent to his neighbor. Because he offends against his neighbor in all sorts of ways he is marked as wicked in God's sight no matter how religious he may think he is. In this instance the wicked is conspicuous by his love of violence.

Does this mean that the Bible repudiates violence without any qualification and always endorses non-violence? We know better. In the world of the Bible, violence can be expressed in such a way that we have to understand it as something more than what God recognizes as a fact (this recognizing is not the same as approving). A careful reading makes it plain that the violence repudiated here is force in the service of injustice. That's why the Hebrew lexicon can render the word in various ways—stressing "injustice" rather than "force." The best rendering I've found is the phrase "violent deed," since everyone will understand this in unfavorable sense.

Militarism

And yet, I don't think this takes us far enough. The expression not only demands our abhorrence because the word "violence" actually means "injustice," but because, in any case, it is violence in the service of injustice. For example, one could assert that the German army was no less guilty of German outrages than was the

Gestapo. But we should not only be on guard against violence
when it's another name for injustice. Quite apart from this we
must be on guard against the *love* of violence, because that's
equally wrong. Literally, the text says: "He (God) hates him who
regards himself wedded to violence." A man must not become in-
fatuated with force even when it's in the service of justice. Anyone who enjoyed the last war, even if he were on the right side,
can be called a militarist and an altogether odious person.

Even God, whose wrath may often be adjudged violence,
doesn't "enjoy" this. He doesn't like to become angry. He knows
what He would rather do! A father who has every reason to give
his son a spanking hates it even when he can't avoid it. It's safe
to say that the Lord God hates it when He has to become angry
with us and "let us have it." We know that "his favor is for a
lifetime," while "his anger is but for a moment" (Ps. 30:5). The
role in which the Lord of heaven and earth most wants to appear
to us is not that of a lion but that of a lamb.

If violence doesn't really suit God, how much more difficult
and painful it ought to be for us who get into it so much more
quickly and eagerly! No wonder that, when it concerns violence,
people hear God speak ironically and tenderly through the prophet
Hosea: "I am God and not man . . ." (Hos. 11:9). No wonder
that God reserves vengeance for Himself instead of leaving it for
others (Rom. 12:19). No wonder that, when He does entrust
force to people, He looks for appointed people in appointed
places (the governing authorities), so that it will not be exercised
arbitrarily or high-handedly (Rom. 13:4). Even government had
better think twice before exercising it, because its force will have
to be used in the service of justice (Ps. 11:7; Rom. 13:4)—and
even then, everything has not been said!

Pacifism

Still, isn't the world of the Old Testament a world of violence?
Indeed. The wars of the Lord even had something akin to what
we today would call total war. The Old Testament includes com-
mandments calling for unparalleled violence, of which a man like

Moses can speak. On the other hand, a man like Jeremiah can give emphatic summons to pacifism and non-violence. The difficulty Christians meet when they appeal to the Bible about war and peace is that they meet both war and peace without equal. This ought to teach both pacifists and non-pacifists to present their points of view less absolutely. In any case, no one today would dare vindicate total war on the basis of the Old Testament. Not because those circumstances belong to a barbaric past—as though the revelation rises or falls with history. No, rather because the circumstances described "lie ahead of us." This applies not only to the severity but also to the gentleness of the Old Testament. On the last day, not only will horses wade through blood up to their stirrups (Rev. 14:20), but the cow and the bear will graze together (Isa. 11:7) and the stormy sea can be walked on as though it were made of glass (Rev. 15:2). If one thing is certain, it's that then force will make an end of violence (cf. the murderers in Revelation 22:15).

Meantime, the world of the Old Testament, as the whole Bible, makes plain that for this present time life without violence is a dream. It's a dream we must always be dreaming—but a dream. And for the simple reason that life without force in the kind of world in which we live would be life without justice—and that would be wicked! It's not only the Moloch of militarism who has slain his millions. The same holds true of the Eros of pacifism. There is a "wicked" antimilitarism ready to hand over the neighbor to the unneighborly—even with very religious phrases. The most we can conclude from the Old Testament, I think, is that life cannot be maintained without some force. That sounds defensive, not aggressive. What is clear from the Old Testament is that we cannot condone violence for the sake of mission, or war for the spread of faith, or an ideology of crusade. Even Israel knew that (Roland de Vaux).

The suffering servant

Violence is always a precarious business. Everyone agrees that violence must not be used for the sake of violence. Militarism has

seldom been guilty of this. But militarism arises when violence is
cherished for the solution of difficult problems between nations,
even if it's not loved for its own sake. We Hollanders think back
to Indonesia, whose former president did not hesitate to employ
violence to solve the problems surrounding New Guinea. I think
we have every right to think of this. But I think we err if we
think that we're free of blame. We too would not have been ready
to reach a settlement had the way of violence not been blocked
for us by our own allies. It's terrible that the Indonesian dictator
assumed nothing could be settled with democratic Holland save by
force of arms. Not only "others" but "we" have to take our text
seriously—that is to say, not only Indonesia but Holland. Nor
may we think only of Russia when we read this Psalm, especially
its line: "if the foundations are destroyed, what can the righteous
do?" In the West, too, we have to learn some things. In the first
place, are the foundations of righteousness so evident among us
that we dare use force in the service of righteousness? In the second place, isn't it possible that force, even in the service of righteousness, will so go to our heads that we'll become fond of it and
so it will become injustice in the service of justice—and may even
crush justice? What Jew and Christian need to learn is that while
the combative servants of the Lord may win fame and do some
good, only the suffering servants of the Lord are the true servants.

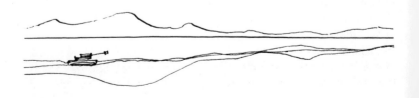

AGAINST THE BIG LIE

*" 'Because the poor are despoiled, because the needy groan,
I will now arise,' says the Lord . . ."*

—Psalm 12:5

How terribly people can lie! It even makes our Psalmist sigh,
"there is no longer any that is godly," which is to say there are no
longer any faithful people left on whom you can depend. We can
take this as a general judgment on a general situation, as a way of
saying, "all men are liars." We can also take it as a judgment
about a particular time that apparently is wholly given over to
lies. There were times when lies followed close on David's heels.
We, too, are acquainted with such times. We think of the way in
which the big lie was in our midst in 1940-1945, the so-called
German time. Again, we may think of the way in which the lie
was used in the Russian time, if I may call it such. I'm thinking
of the Hungarian lie and of the Czechoslovakian lie.

This kind of folk doesn't lie about it

This is not to say that "all cats are gray." Times of extraordinary falsehood presuppose, both before and after, times of fidelity
to truth. And they must also reckon with people who oppose the
spirit of the time. During the German time we thought the Allies
spoke the truth, and we like to believe that the West tells the
truth in the "Russian" time. Even the poet's ominous expression,
"there is no longer any that is godly," presupposes that there is at
least one who is such—the poet himself. Even if we take "all men

are liars" in the most general sense, it presupposes that the speaker doesn't lie—at any rate not as much as the rest.

How can I be sure that in one way or other I don't do it—at any rate not as much as the rest? Why can't we dismiss the poet as a Pharisee, to name only one notorious liar?

That's obvious. What folks don't lie about the situation but instead are oppressed by it? They're the wretched and the poor. Precisely these are the folk with whom the poet identifies himself. Real Pharisees are usually neither wretched nor poor. But this kind of folk doesn't "lie about it."

What is lying?

This provides the clue as to what lying really is, and why it has rather little to do with "telling a fib." No respectable person tells a fib, but lying—and that's our concern—doesn't stop with respectability.

Our Psalm not only speaks of falsehood as about the worst thing there is: in the same breath it fulminates against the oppressions of the wretched and the groaning of the poor. We have to conclude that these are not two different things but that one is included in the other. The big lie becomes the lie against love, which is the same as lovelessness.

It's not only this Psalm which makes us aware of this relationship. We meet it all through the Bible. In John 8:44, for example, the devil is called both a murderer and a liar from the beginning. Apparently that's one and the same. In his first epistle, the same John equates truth and love, falsehood and lovelessness. To take another striking example, when Ananias and Sapphira cheated with love, they discover that they had lied (Acts 5:3).

That makes us uneasy. Who were the liars during the German time? Certainly the Germans who equated a new order with gas ovens for Jews and catastrophic oppression of the wretched and groaning of the poor. But what of those who didn't lift a hand to stop it, to deter it, to oppose it? Who are the big liars today? Bolsheviks who twist the bloodiest facts? Certainly. But doesn't the map of the West have places enough where the wretched are

being oppressed and where the poor groan? Think of Spain, of
Portugal, of South Africa, of Greece. Where is there such wide-
spread and callous divorce—in other words, where is there so
much departure from love—as among ourselves? We'd better not
excuse this with brave words about freedom and justice lest the
poet accuse us of double-mindedness, of glib tongues, of boasting,
and of belonging to the company of those who prevail with their
tongues (vs. 4). That's who we are more than ever before
through newspaper and radio!

East and West

East and West can tell lies with the best because East and West
have lovelessness to spare. Verse 2 of our Psalm hits both camps.
What a lying, loveless mess there is on earth!

That's why the church never identified itself with the Allied
camp, though it certainly thought it appropriate for its members
to wage war against the German camp. Similarly, the church will
take care now not to identify itself with the West. The West, too,
is much too deceitful and loveless for the church to do this—even
if the difference between East and West lies in the fact that the
West offers the church more opportunity to unmask lies and to
fight lovelessness. The church had better identify itself with the
"poor" and the "wretched" both inside and outside the Iron Curtain. In any case, those who are called "blessed" in the Bible—
and they're as many as the sands of the sea and the stars of the
sky—are the poor in spirit, those who mourn, the meek, those
who hunger after righteousness, and those who are persecuted
(Matt. 5:3-6, 10).

Cross and resurrection

Does this mean more than that sympathetic and compassionate
words be addressed by the church to the poor?

Yes, it means more. It means neither more nor less than that the
Word of God wants to address them—and that Word is more
than sympathetic and compassionate. The only Word which is

wholly pure, which wholly means what it says, which specifically wants to live with the poor and the wretched, the only Word which really is love is the Word that wants to come and did come in Jesus Christ. What else does the incarnation mean? His faithfulness wanted to refine this word not seven times but seventy times seven—in the smelting furnace of Golgotha.

Jesus Christ has so identified Himself with the poor and wretched that He appeared the most poor and wretched of all when He hung on the cross. However, I'm not only thinking of the cross. I'm thinking also of the resurrection. I do so because the Psalm says quite literally: " 'Because the poor are despoiled, because the needy groan, I will now arise,' says the LORD . . ." We know how this word has become reality. We also know with what effect—for the guards "became like dead men" (Matt. 28:4).

The only Lord

And yet the Psalm ends in bewilderment. What do we see after having heard all these happy tidings? That the wicked still trot about as cheerfully as they did at the outset! It looks as though nothing has changed, as though they are still lord and master, as though lying and lovelessness have eternal life.

For that matter, when the Lord rose in the midst of His enemies and when Easter was first celebrated, the Pharisees (as we know from the Book of Acts) still trotted about as cheerfully as ever. As though nothing had happened! And yet they couldn't hinder a message which has lodged in our heart stubbornly and doggedly, a message that has broken through and with Him has been set free out of the lovelessness of death—call it the faith that the meek shall inherit the earth (Matt. 5:5).

It's not only the Christian who has a lease on this knowledge. The Psalmist had it already, as has the Jew of every age. Even though the big liars have done their best to pilfer that knowledge, the Jew, in the face of death pit and gas oven has borne witness that the Lord, the God of Israel, is the only Lord and the only Redeemer—our last and only chance. Surely a Christian cannot do less.

DOUBT AND TRUST

"How long, O Lord?"

—Psalm 13:1

The Bible is acquainted with our questions and doubts—and not only the Psalms. Take Habakkuk 1:2: "O LORD, how long shall I cry for help, and thou wilt not hear? Or cry to thee 'Violence!' and thou wilt not save?" Still, it's especially true of the Psalms. The preceding Psalms have already manifested such doubt (9:19; 10:12). Here it's especially serious, for the question "How long, O LORD?" is followed by the fell cry "Wilt thou forget me for ever?" The words "for ever" stand out, while afterward we hear that it drags on day after day. That is to say, every day the poet thought there would at last be an end to it, but every day the questions and doubts return.

Modern

All this sounds very modern. While the climate of thought described here is not atheism in the modern sense of the word, it certainly savors of something that nowadays we call the absence of God. Modern atheism is unknown in the world of the Psalms. It has little to do with questions and doubts because it has no *address* for them. But the absence of God, the hidden God—how disturbing is this about One of whom we always think not in terms of concealment but of revelation! We're bothered by this and we nurse all kinds of ideas about it, just as the poet did. Think of the books we read or write about it. Think of the study guides and the study weeks devoted to it by this or that Christian braintrust. Why does all this help so precious little? How long?

Doubt as the enemy

Whence comes this doubt? Who or what causes it? The text tells us plainly. It's the enemy, the "familiar" enemy in the Psalms and in the life of the believer—the enemy who reveals himself so personally that he is called "my" enemy.

Who or what is this enemy of mine? We have to answer this in circular fashion. The enemy is everything and anything that sows doubt in my heart. If we wish we may consider the Russians the enemy, but we have to consider quite as much the armaments race that tries to keep this enemy at a distance. We may think of the flood in Spain some years ago that carried away hundreds of people who had been praying fervently for rain, never dreaming that when it came it would come as a murderer. We may think of the problem this kind of answered prayer poses. We may think of someone who speaks all too glibly about God. We may think of all this and more. Some commentators have taken the word "shaken" in verse 4 as a dread eye disease. While we can dismiss this as farfetched, it's not farfetched to suppose that something like that can become the occasion for doubt. Not seldom a bit of pain can hide God from us.

That doubt is a strong enemy is freely admitted. At a given moment the Psalmist is completely cast down while his adversary rejoices. Seen in this light, one wouldn't give much for faith—not when temptation can call the tune.

Classical

Apparently doubt is not as modern as we like to suppose. Thousands of years ago, people evidently were acquainted with it in the history of faith. So much the worse for them—but so much the more reassuring for us now! At any rate, it should help us to be more sober in our temptations, to show off less, and to sing about it in lower key. For that matter, the Psalms can tell us of other things we like to think are peculiarly modern but were always present. For example, take modern art. Why call the poet classical if he says the cedars of Lebanon can dance and the rivers clap their hands—and then call Picasso modern when he paints this for us? Both are equally modern or classical or both. Perhaps it's better to say that there's no modern art. There's only good and bad art. However, that's not what it's about here. Of course there's a peculiarly modern kind of doubt, just as art always portrays its own time and has to do so (W. Sandberg). But doubt itself is not modern. It's as old as the fall of man. It's classical.

All men are doubters

Speaking of paradise can carry us a bit further. There we see how devilish question and doubt can be (Gen. 3:1). We mustn't cover this up with nice words as though it were an innocent affair, or as though we understood it all. To do so would be poor service to a real doubter. At bottom doubt is something that must be fought because it comes from the devil. It must not become fashionable.

It doesn't only come from the devil. That would be too easy! Doubt also comes from people. It comes from wicked people who say, as in Psalm 10, "God has forgotten, he has hidden his face, he will never see it" (cf. Ps. 14:1).

It frightens us to notice that these are the very words echoed by our poet. It follows that doubt doesn't just come from specifically wicked people. All men can talk this way. Shall we conclude that we can't always distinguish clearly between the wicked and the other people, since all men are a bit wicked, a race of doubters? Undoubtedly (Ps. 14:1-2).

What a surprise!

However, the story of man's fall in paradise can teach us something else. It can teach us that the real question is not "Where are you, Lord?"—as we hear this question posed by the poet or by

ourselves. The real question is "Where are you, Adam?" (Gen.
3:9). In any case, the latter question precedes the former, and the
former is impossible without the latter. God is hidden because
men hide. Even so, the way He hides Himself can be called a
"moment" compared with the way we hide ourselves. "For a brief
moment I forsook you, but with great compassion I will gather
you" (Isa. 54:7).

To put it positively, doubt has had it! Even though it may not
appear so, even though it appears to be "thorns and thistles" forever (Gen. 3:18), even though our heel may be bruised, the ser-
pent's head has had it (Gen. 3:15)! What a surprise!

That's the surprise with which the Psalm's close confronts us.
After all the poet has said, we wouldn't have thought he would
say, "But I . . ." It comes very suddenly, not dull or sour but
jubilant. The enemy has met his match. Doubt has met its match
in trust.

A question of trusting

How does the man get this so quickly? Apparently it's a matter
of trusting, as the text adds immediately. Such trust seems enormous. In the midst of doubt we hear the poet say that the Lord
has dealt bountifully with him. We would say all this still has to
happen ("How long, O LORD?"), but the poet has looked beyond
the boundary of his doubt and reckons the present by the future.
We're reminded of another poet, John on Patmos, who in the
midst of blood and fire and smoking vapor was able to write of
the glorious things revealed to him—of the end of tears and
death, sorrow and weeping and trouble, indeed of all that causes
doubt—"It *is* done!" (Rev. 21:6).

That's strong language about strong examples—of a great Jew
and of a great Christian. However, we still haven't met the strongest language and example. That comes from a man who, when He
still had to begin His victory, when Gethsemane and Golgotha
were still ahead of Him, could say already, ". . . be of good
cheer, I have overcome the world" (John 16:33). Surely he was
the greatest Jew and the first Christian, Jesus Christ.

We might be frightened by such strong language and example. Do we have to duplicate and imitate this? True enough—but to say this is not enough. Jesus Christ isn't simply the greatest Jew and the first Christian. He's not only fully man but fully God. That is to say, He hasn't simply said all this before us. He's also and especially said it to us.

We can put it like this. To trust is something a man lays on God, but it's also and especially something that God has laid on man.

WHAT REALLY IS ATHEISM?

*"The fool says in his heart,
'There is no God.'"*

—Psalm 14:1

Atheists say, "There is no God." According to the Bible, not only atheists say this, but also the "fool." Does this allow us to conclude that today's atheism is simply extreme foolishness, that we can simply dismiss as ignoramus anyone who says he doesn't believe in God? Or is this too ridiculous? To be sure, I think, it may be the case sometimes. A person may actually be too stupid to believe in God. I don't mean too stupid in the intellectual sense of the word. I mean too stupid in the existential sense of the word. That is to say, a person can be too lazy, too little alive, to be able to believe in God. Let's not hedge—it can happen. Generally speaking, however, we'd better think twice before we dismiss someone as a fool because he doesn't believe in God. He may have good reason!

Is atheism so foolish?

Atheism is always a complicated matter—at least as complicated as nihilism. That the latter is a complicated matter is evident in Professor P. Smit's inaugural address at Leiden which has the significant title *In Search of Nihilism*. The title indicates that he isn't sure who or what a nihilist is, or whether one really exists!

Originally the term "nihilism" was a term of honor, comparable with the word *"geus"* [1] among Hollanders. However, the latter was originally a term of abuse (= beggar) which became a title of honor, whereas "nihilist" was originally a title of honor which later became a term of abuse. In his novel *Fathers and Sons,* the Russian author Turgenev uses nihilism in its original sense. In this novel, written about the middle of the last century, the most attractive figure is a nihilist. Nihilism means here a view of life held by those who believe in nothing (= nihil) so long as there is such crying injustice to neighbor as was the case in the Russia of the last century. The nihilists of that time were also atheists. They cared "nothing" about the God in whom their Russia believed. We can hardly blame them. Was the one in whom people believed really God? Surely He wasn't the God of whom we sing:

> The people's poor ones he shall judge,
> the needy's children save;
> And those shall he in pieces break
> who them oppressed have.
> (Psalm 72, *The Scottish Psalter*)

Were such people not right to refuse to believe in a God who obviously wasn't the God of the Bible anymore but a false god? Is atheism really always so foolish?

God and the gods

At least they were right to the extent that, when someone says, "No, I don't believe in God," we ought to ask first, "In what God don't you believe?" Maybe we should congratulate him for his atheism instead of expressing condolence, let alone thinking we should attack him! It could well be that he has rejected an erroneous idea of God which was forced on him by his parents, his environment, his social class, even his church. If so, he hasn't re-

---

1. TRANSLATOR'S NOTE: *"Geus"* means "beggar." At the beginning of the Dutch revolt against Spain in the sixteenth century, influential noblemen and burghers banded themselves together in 1566 to present a protest against grievances. The Spanish regent's advisers scoffed, "What, Madam? Is your Highness afraid of these beggars [*ces gueux*]?" The opponents responded by calling themselves "Beggars," taking the symbols of common begging, the wallet and bowl.

jected true worship but has turned away from the worship of false images or even of false gods. Who is to say how much of the atheism of the previous century arose because in a religion that sanctioned militarism, capitalism, and colonialism, men no longer could find traces of the God of Israel who is concerned with peace and with the poor and with all nations?

Conversion

Of course, we congratulate someone not because he doesn't believe in God, but because he doesn't believe in a false god. It might be our opportunity to point him to the true God. That one doesn't want to believe in a false god is no excuse for not believing in the true God. Christendom's faults don't excuse a person for not becoming a Christian. That's the more true since a perfect Christendom and a "pure culture" never existed and never will. Church, Christendom, and faith include a grab bag of motives, including some very bad ones. An atheist should be able to recognize and understand this. He only needs to be married. Marriage too includes a grab bag of motives, some of which are not very pretty.

But that's up to the atheist. For us it should mean conversion. It means the conversion of all sorts of ideas about God that only harden or provoke the world in its atheism. It means the conversion of all sorts of ideas of God for which the Bible has no place. For example, it means the conversion of ideas that suffocate the neighbor because they are so antisocial, so white, so Western.

Atheism and atheism

That's why atheism is a complicated matter. Is that so in our Psalm? There it seems to be perfectly clear and simple. There it's said that atheism is too foolish to run scot-free!

Maybe so. But the atheism attacked here is not "our" atheism, not modern unbelief. It has nothing in common with this for the simple reason that it wasn't present inside or outside Israel. Doubt, yes—we saw that in the previous Psalm. But today's atheism is characterized precisely by its lack of doubt. The world of the Old Testament is a world of Jews and Gentiles—but the Gentile world too is not exactly a world of unbelief. One could describe it rather as a world that believed dreadfully much—far too much! Our text reproaches people who believe but who take their belief for granted. From the way in which they deal with their neighbor it's evident that they don't really believe. The God of the Bible is the God of our neighbor.

Wickedness is always linked with unneighborliness. This is fully described in Psalm 10, where the wicked is called a usurer, one who curses his neighbor, a deceiver, an oppressor, a man of unrighteousness who preys on the weak and murders the innocent and traps the wretched. We notice the same in Psalm 14. The wicked are people who commit cruel and abominable crimes. They devour their fellowmen as "they eat bread," and they're truly workers of unrighteousness.

This is the kind of atheism of which a believer, a church member, is capable. The church member often acts as though God doesn't exist by acting as though his neighbor doesn't exist.

With what consequence? Today's unbeliever will think a thousand times before he becomes a believer. And that has a further consequence. Today's believer should think a thousand times before he decides to inveigh against an atheist. Generally speaking, at least, this is true.

Understandable but incomprehensible

Once more. How does a person, a people, or a culture decide to become atheistic? In the case of Russia it's quite understandable. In the previous century Christian Russia had the opportunity to let God be seen by loving the neighbor and lifting the oppressed as He does. It failed to do so. The church of Eastern Europe formerly acted a-socially by allying itself with a-social regimes. Again, how can we expect conversion to the true God in Red China today when the former Christian regime behaved so shamefully in His name? Atheism is quite understandable.

At least among unbelievers—and that's what it's about here!

But how do believers measure up in their own behavior? That's incomprehensible. That's not even a question mark; that's guilt, pure and simple. That's too foolish to run scot-free because that's the "purest" wickedness. Compared with this, the anti-God propaganda in Moscow doesn't amount to anything. Russian atheism may have slain it tens of thousands, but the atheism of Christendom has slain its millions.

Justification of the ungodly

In view of this a question might arise: "In that case, who isn't an athetist?" In point of fact, our Psalm answers, "They have all gone astray, they are all alike corrupt; there is none that does good, no, not one." As he broods over the wickedness of which believers are capable, the Psalmist doesn't dare excuse anyone, including himself. "No, not one." Paul must have quoted these words for the same reasons—because he couldn't exempt anyone, whether Greek or Jew, world or church (as we would say). No one is exempt. When we examine closely, what an ungodly mess there is in the world.

But notice where Paul says this. He says it in his letter to the Romans. That tells us something more. That letter was not written to reproach the ungodly. Even though these are not spared, the letter to the Romans has become famous not for its reproach but for its justification of the ungodly (Rom. 4:5). Since Luther, we know this to be the heart of the letter. It's also the heart of our Psalm (14:7)!

CHURCHGOING

"O Lord, who shall sojourn in thy tent?"

—Psalm 15:1

In this Psalm the regulations or rather the conditions of churchgoing are discussed. The words "tent" and "holy hill" make us think of what we call "church." Moreover, the song has all the characteristics of a pilgrim song sung by those who stand at the threshold of the holy place. Who may enter? Who may come to church? According to this Psalm, it simply isn't true that everyone is welcome—as we like to tell ourselves and anyone else who will listen. Nothing doing! We have to keep the rules!

Ethics and liturgy

Someone may observe that what we hear in this Psalm has more to do with ethics than with worship. That's a misunderstanding. If we look carefully, there's no dilemma—certainly not in the Psalms. What songs are so wholly cultic and suited for worship—wholly liturgical? Again, what songs have such a series of regulations for living—wholly ethical? Evidently the one doesn't exclude the other. In other words, the best ethic makes for the best worship.

It can be done

Someone may suggest that this is enough to scare him to death. Such demands! And he's right. It's not only in this Psalm that these demands confront us. That happens in many Psalms. For example, Psalm 24 approaches our Psalm in seriousness and severity. But we must admit that nowhere does it seem to frighten us more than here.

After reading and reflecting on this Psalm, we might be tempted to answer the question "who shall sojourn in thy tent?" with a quick "Not I!" And we might add, "Nor anyone else!" Then suddenly we remember something or rather someone, and we say, "Only Christ." Jesus Christ is the only one who could keep this list of regulations. He's the only one who did. He can sojourn in God's tent.

While preparing a sermon on this text along this line, I was telling my wife about it. She took vigorous exception, convinced that this line of thought was a detour. She thought it was *escape* for someone just to lay his difficulties on Jesus when he found them too hard—a pious escape. She also had some further reflections. She thought it was the way of least resistance, not so much a *pious* way as an *escape*—the escape of a person who thinks he can use Jesus Christ for everything, and therefore can be criticized as misusing Him. Her point was that the Psalm was concerned with "to do." I think she was right.

To be sure, Jesus Christ is a splendid portrait that catches the eye. But He's also a splendid example. He did it "for us" but He also did it "before us." He is both portrait and pattern. We must follow Him. Such language as that of the poet is about *doing*. That's why we need to examine these rules more closely.

So many things

The first word we meet is "blamelessly." In fact, we almost stumble over it. What the poet means is made clear in Psalm 19:13. "Blameless" doesn't mean "perfect," but "free from presumptuous sins." We might be inclined to think God doesn't shear us too closely or look too closely. We might even be tempted to ask whether He's a relativist—not because He's a poor ethicist but because no one else is so merciful as He.

There's something to this. One could argue that no one looks at us less closely than God. But one can also argue the reverse. Let's not forget that the poet of Psalm 19, who understands "blameless" as "free from presumptuous sins," has just prayed God to forgive his "hidden" sins. N. H. Ridderbos understands "blameless" not as "sinlessness but as receiving forgiveness after praying about hidden sins and trusting in God's power to guard against falling." Let's keep this in mind. It means that we must not go too far in sin if we go to church. For that matter, who would want to do both?

As for going too far, we can take this in several ways. It means, for example, that we ought to do what's right. Wouldn't it be the last straw if we didn't? We ought to speak the truth. Isn't that obvious? Of course we should—"from [the] heart." We ought to speak the truth and mean it. Who would deny this? Who would suggest that the church doesn't take seriously what it understands to be the truth? Is that possible?

The following verse is concerned with one thing—we must not slander. Who wants to do that? The verse—or rather, the church —hinges on the phrase "his friend." Who is that? In the Old Testament he's the fellow countryman, and in the New Testament he's the fellow believer. He deserves our unfeigned attention. But not only he. In Galatians 6:10, we read that we must "do good to all men" as well as "especially to those who are of the household of faith." If this is so, who isn't our "friend"? What does this say to our world today where white and brown, European and Asian, East and West are next-door neighbors? White and brown, European and Asian, East and West had better see to it that what they promise each other doesn't become slander—and the church on both sides had better take the lead. What church wouldn't want to do this? On the other hand, doesn't the beginning of verse 4 sound pharisaical when we're told to despise and look down our nose? Quite the contrary. After all, who or what is the "reprobate" we are to despise? It's the despiser. In other words, the only people whom we may and must despise are themselves despisers. To do this is to "fear the LORD"!

The last part of verse 4 can raise problems for one who thinks of the pledges made between Holland and New Guinea. Those pledges were not kept—at least not as they were made and understood. Many Hollanders felt that we could and even had to go back on our pledge to Papua because they no longer believed this pledge would serve independence but would rather make for isolation from neighboring Indonesia. The Dutch churches, in their insistence on reconciliation and avoidance of war, rightly felt that they were within the spirit of this verse in doing so.

For me the meaning of the last verse seems the most difficult. We cannot simply take this as a direct command forbidding interest because the prohibition of usury in Israel functioned in a world where interest was tantamount to extortion—i.e., 20-40%. (The Hebrew word used here means "to bite"!) With a variation of Matthew 5:34, we would be able to say: "But I say to you, take no interest at all." If this verse poses a question mark for the world of commerce to the extent that this is a cruel world, it poses a question mark particularly for believers who have business dealings with each other. Might not Paul's insistence that church members should not take each other to court (1 Cor. 6:1) have something to say here? I simply raise this as a question. For the rest, the meaning is plain enough. The person who goes to church must be ready to live with such questions when he is in business, and he must avoid dirty practices like the plague.

Nothing extraordinary

Not to go too far, to do justice, to speak the truth and mean it, not to slander the neighbor, to despise only the despisers, to do good, to keep promises when these are right, to watch out for Mammon—all this is demanded of the church. When we look closely at these, there's nothing extraordinary about them. We expect all this not only of the church. Every decent man stands or falls with this. It's a demand for decency—nothing more and nothing less.

Should someone observe that the rules go beyond outward to inward decency (there's mention of the "heart") and so there is something extraordinary here, it's not really extraordinary. We know this from the Sermon on the Mount, of which this Psalm reminds us. In neither is anything said about faith (unless one can prove it by the way in which the question is put). If someone insists that Jesus demanded more than the ordinary of his disciples (Matt.5:47), we must reply that precisely this "extraordinary" is "not extraordinary" for a believer. It's simply the obvious!

The whole context

Accordingly, he who keeps as regulation and sees all this as the rule of life can go to church and receive the promise. We're not talking here of exceptions which we've all made to this list from time to time when we fall shamefully short. Thank God, that need not mean we're no longer welcome in the holy place. Witness David, the poet of many Psalms, who could fall terribly short but who also could confirm this rule zealously. Such a person may go to church and receive the promise. He "shall never be moved."

Because the Psalm begins as it does, we might have expected the poet to say he may "dwell" in God's tent instead of saying that he may never be moved. Yet it really comes down to the same thing. To go to church is to go to a kind of bunker.

We must examine this more carefully. What precisely does it mean "not to be moved"? To avoid misunderstanding, it has nothing to do with the notion that those who go to church will never be anxious. Psalm 91, for example, is anxious through and through—filled with snares, plagues, lions and bears on the road, and snakes in the grass. Nonetheless, there too mention is made of "not being moved" and of "coming through." That is to say, the church will make it! In other words, "the gates of hell will not prevail against it" (Matt. 16:18, K.J.V.). Perhaps we'd better say, not any church but the church that holds on to Psalm 15 will make it!

Will the church only be guarded physically or also morally? That really doesn't make much difference. Of course, it will be preserved morally. When the church understands churchgoing in terms of the regulations in this Psalm, not only will it be bound by God through them, it will be preserved by God in them in blessed manner. We know this relationship, this perfect relationship, in the perfect prayer: "And forgive us our debts, as we forgive our debtors." Where the former happens, the latter happens also.

Perhaps the best way to check all this is through some words from the Epistle to the Hebrews. How do we come to the holy place? How do we come to church? We read: "by the blood of Jesus" (Heb. 10:19). However, we must examine more precisely what "not to be moved" means. "Strive for peace with all men, and for the holiness without which no one will see the Lord" (Heb. 12:14). Without this we won't make it into the church! The whole context becomes plain when we read Hebrews 13:1-5: "Let brotherly love continue. Do not neglect to show hospitality to strangers, for thereby some have entertained angels unawares. Remember those who are in prison, as though in prison with them; and those who are ill-treated, since you also are in the body. Let marriage be held in honor among all, and let the marriage bed be undefiled; for God will judge the immoral and adulterous. Keep your life free from love of money, and be content with what you have." And then we also hear: "for he has said, 'I will never fail you nor forsake you.' "

THE QUESTION ABOUT THE GOOD

"I have no good apart from thee"

—Psalm 16:2

For the poet the question about the good is wholly bound up with God. Considering the circumstances in which he finds himself, we have to admit that he's well advised to do so. When we hear him sigh, "Preserve me, O God," and note from what follows that he's confronted with death and the grave, we infer that the circumstances in which he wrote these lines were hazardous indeed. This isn't contradicted by what we read in verse 6: "The lines have fallen for me in pleasant places." In view of the previous verse, it's hard to think this heritage is anything or anyone other than God Himself. Accordingly, we conclude that of course this man seeks the good in God alone since he simply has no opportunity of finding it anywhere else. It's like someone about to die. Everything else in life that might be called good disappears. He has no choice—except God alone.

A world turned upside down

This conclusion is a bit unjust and hasty. After all, in the world of our poet, besides God, there are doubtless false gods enough who bid for attention in times of danger. These, like all false gods, at first sight are not repulsive but winsome and attractive. If we can believe N. H. Ridderbos, the Netherlands Bible Society has mistranslated. He thinks verse 3 doesn't describe those who with the poet have been able to keep the false gods at a distance —the so-called "saints" and "noble"—but that it's the false gods who appear in this light! They are in the odor of sanctity and glory. They offer us the most religious illusions. They caress our well-being—whether they be the false gods of the past or the securities of today. So impressive is their appearance, so eagerly sought their presence, that we can speak of a world turned upside down. What verse 4 calls "bidding for the favor of" actually means "giving a bridal gift." That's really an upside-down world because the gift is given to, instead of by, the lover (to the bride).

A lucky number

That this is an upside-down world is evident also in the consequences. The false gods appear to demand more than they give. Indeed, they're all demand. They're all sorrow, we could add with the poet who has experienced them.

On the other hand, the true God gives more than He demands. Indeed, He's all gift, all surprise. On love's terrain one could speak as though he's drawn a lucky number. I don't think I'm popularizing verses 5 and 6 too much when I say that the one true God actually appears as a lucky number when contrasted with the false gods who demand our blood, which is to say, our existence.

For Christ's sake

What if we don't feel ourselves and our good in jeopardy, as did our poet? Do we have to give up the good life we enjoy for the sake of "God only"—good health, wife and children, good folk around us who may or may not be Christians? No, that's not the meaning at all. Not only is God called good in the Bible, but people are called good, whether Christian or not. What value the Bible attaches to people being good (and not bad) is seen in the fact that no less than the governing authorities have received God's commission to maintain this antithesis with the sword

(Rom. 13:4). Paul tells us this, but Jesus also distinguishes between the bad and the good (Matt. 12:35). Nor is the predicate "good" only applied to people. It's applied to heaven and earth, to plants and animals and more. "And God saw everything that he had made, and behold, it was very good" (Gen. 1:31).

We can and must include even the pagan world, for we read that "the glory and the honor of the nations" are heartily welcome in the new Jerusalem.

This takes us a bit farther. It shows that this eternal preservation of what may and must be called good, quite apart from faith in God, this preservation under a new heaven and on a new earth is not outside God because it's not outside Christ. After all, who knew how to melt the Lord God's heart so that His wrath melted to a river of the water of life, on which the new earth with all its good forever depends (Rev. 22:1)? Who else but His Son!

Meanwhile, we haven't yet come, or no longer come, to the time when the good is given free. As long as this is so, we do well to shelter our good in God—be it health, wife and children, desire or enjoyment. If we don't, all these, no matter how "holy" and "glorious," easily become idolatry. Nor is this the only reason. How quickly our happiness can be eaten away today as indeed in any age between the first and the last day. What comfort it is then to remember that there's no good without God and that only He knows the mystery and meaning of who and what is really good.

Good Friday

He knows this so well that even in the midst of what we would (rightly) call unmitigated evil, He is able to make something good, something very good.

We could give various examples of how "good" it was for me to have been "afflicted" (Ps. 119:75). Examples can be drawn from personal experience and from world history (or should we call it salvation history?). I think of the terrible evil done to the Jews in the thirties and forties. Except for the wave of sympathy this brought to a world of anti-Semitism, I don't think the good of the state of Israel would have happened. That must never mean that the Lord God does the evil as well as the good, nor that He does the former for the sake of the latter. What a cruel harmony that would be! Rather it means that when He stumbles over the former He not only stumbles over it but picks it up and graciously knows how to do something great and surprising with it.

Israel always had an awareness of this. Few things experienced by the Jew were so evil to him as death. Yet even of death our Psalmist can testify that his soul will not be "abandoned" in it. We must not read back into this too quickly the idea of resurrection as Christians know this. Yet we can't help noticing that, if the poet is David (and why not?), the hope raised in verse 10 was at least fulfilled to the extent that he died in old age and so was spared direct confrontation with death for many years. A believer is here expressing his faith that God is able to do something good even with something as evil as death. Exactly what he didn't know— but, to be honest, neither do we. We're not able to unlock the revelation of this mystery.

No, we can't, either. We can say that a corner of the veil has been lifted—even that a whole curtain has been rent (Luke 23:45). A Christian belives that he has participated in the most astonishing reversal of evil to good, because the worst Friday in world history is henceforth celebrated as Good Friday. There's a big difference between the good that befell the Jew of Psalm 16 and that which befell the Jew of Golgotha. That's made clear in Acts 13:35-36, where we read that David, in the strict sense of the word, "saw corruption" while Jesus Christ did not. That's why verse 10 of our Psalm has become truth for Him in a very particular way.

No good apart from God

And not only for Him! He is yet only "the first fruits of those who have fallen asleep" (1 Cor. 15:20). For the time being God still must make good out of evil, and we must test the good in the evil and can never wholly rely on the good, since at any moment it can turn to evil. But this will not always be so.

One day we will not need to find shelter in Him. One day we

won't need to question Him about the good. For to those who have sought first the Kingdom of God—that is, have sought Him —it will be added (Matt. 6:33). Then it will be given free and will no longer be a question because "death shall be no more, neither shall there be mourning nor crying nor pain" (Rev. 21:4).

Then, too, the tent of God will still be near (Rev. 21:3), though less as shelter than as festive hall! Then we will know for certain that without God our good is no longer good. Left to itself it falls in ruins (Matt. 19:17). If the Son, albeit in His humiliation, could say, "Why do you call me good? No one is good but God alone" (Luke 18:19)—then a man, albeit in his exaltation, had better cling to that.

ON BEING SATISFIED

"As for me, I shall behold thy face in righteousness;
when I awake, I shall be satisfied with beholding thy form."

—Psalm 17:15

What makes faith so exciting, such a mountain climb, such an ocean voyage, such an adventure, such a vista? Isn't that why we believe—because that's what faith is like? There's always something new. For the church, too, that's what holds suspense and love. By love, says Antoine de Saint-Exupéry, we don't mean that we're to look at each other, but that we look in the same direction together. In what direction and on whom is the church never tired of looking?

What an image!

What is said at the close of the Psalm is its climax. We never tire of looking at the form of God. And why not? What kind of form is it and what kind of God? It's the form of a God who hears "a just cause," who attends our cry, who hears our prayer, who listens to "lips free of deceit." He's the address for all right that can't receive its right, and for all sorrow that doesn't know what to do with its sorrow. He's the address for every envelope filled with complaints. Tremendous! What an image!

On the side of the fat

The address for every envelope and for every complaint? No. He's not the address for every matter, nor does He have an an-

swer for every lip. We've said that He's the address for every just
cause and for every lip free of deceit.

Accordingly, God isn't the address for every Christian, but only
for Christians who hold fast to just causes. Here we should not
only think of people in business. Isn't everyone "in business" one
way or other in the world? Just causes will not seldom be persecuted, despised, scorned, unpopular, and oppressed causes. We
can take the language of verse 4 and say that a Christian is one
who in the world doesn't stand on the side of the world. He's not
on the side of the bootlickers, no matter how polished! Or again,
in the language of verse 10, a Christian is one who isn't "inclosed
in [his] own fat" (K.J.V.). The expression speaks for itself. It suggests slickness, self-sufficiency. We'd better watch out. It's not just
communists who side with force and oppression—and whatever
else we may want to say about them. At least they don't often
stand "on the side of the fat."

How is it possible?

How can anyone use such strong language about himself as this
poet does? How can anyone claim his own affairs are righteous
and his own lips are free of deceit? How can anyone dare tell God
to test his heart, and be confident He will find nothing wrong—
even when our meditations are set free and toss about without
restraint at night? How can anyone dare God to put him under a
magnifying glass with such clear conscience? Can such a person
really be a Christian? Isn't he more apt to be a fashion-fop?

Such a person *must* be a Christian. Such a thing *must* be possible. Maybe not completely, surely not completely—after all, faith
is not perfectionism—but thank God, now and then, here and
there, in particular situations it must be possible. Our Psalm
speaks of this in a particular situation and not in general terms.

Grace isn't cheap

We must not be so nervous about good works. We must rather
put our shoulder to it. We must not be afraid of becoming "Ro-

man Catholic" or "pharisaical." Better to be more afraid of being
so afraid of good works and of becoming "Roman Catholic" or
"pharisaical." Better to be more afraid of the "Roman Catholic"
question in the Heidelberg Catechism: "But does not this teaching
make people careless and sinful?" Better to be more afraid of the
commandment in Matthew 5: ". . . unless your righteousness exceeds that of the scribes and Pharisees . . ."

The "proud" tone of our Psalm isn't meant to be frightening
but liberating. It liberates us from that servile civility whereby
Christians think they do God a service by endlessly rehearsing
how vile and worthless they are. What a hypocritical humility,
what a "good work" in the worst sense of the word is this fear of
good works! The Psalm liberates us from this sort of God-damned
inertia whereby we accomplish nothing. Our Psalm calls us to the
opposite of all this. It calls us to look for just causes in the world,
for a just politics, for a just society. It calls for people, groups,
and parties that will not side with violence, with the big mouth,
with the big bootlickers and the fat. It calls us to side with the
oppressed.

Once more. Is this stout talk not typically Old Testament—
"Look, Lord God, I've done my best"? No. Paul too can say that
he "always" took pains to have "a clean conscience toward God
and toward men" (Acts 24:16). He wasn't thinking only of his
own background. He too helps us recover what we're most apt to
stumble over—the "as for me" of verse 5. After describing the
Gentile world Paul says to believers, "But you are altogether different" (cf. Eph. 4:20). And where shall we find a more exact
paraphrase of our Psalm than in the words of Jesus (Matt. 5:8):
"Blessed are the pure in heart [cf. vss. 1-14], for they shall see
God" (vs. 15)? No, this language isn't typically Old Testament;
it's typically biblical. It liberates us from the worst thing there is,
cheap grace (the big swindle).

Grace? Is the Psalm concerned with grace instead of merit? Yes
indeed. Isn't our lack of guilt also a matter of grace? To avoid
any misunderstanding, this Psalm (as though intentionally) is
called a *prayer*. Only three Psalms are so named (Pss. 17, 90,

102), though in fact there are many more. When prayer is mentioned grace is meant. It has to be so.

The great love

We must go back a moment to where we began—to that form at which the poet, when he awakes, never tires of looking. What is meant by this awakening?

First of all, he surely means what happened to each of us this morning. As in the case of Psalm 16:10, we must not think too quickly of resurrection but simply of waking up each morning. As if such a tremendous event is ordinary! Doesn't each new morning have something tremendous about it—of God and man going together in search of adventure, the adventure of righteousness?

Only then may we look for something beyond this, as we did in Psalm 16:10. Only then may we begin to think of the great awakening on the last day when we shall be satisfied with the form of God or, what is actually the same thing, with the great righteousness. That awakening will be the day when there will be no more death, "neither . . . mourning nor crying nor pain" (Rev. 21:4). Only then, as in 1 Corinthians 13:12, will I "understand fully, even as I have been fully understood." We can take the latter to mean "to love as I have been fully loved." Sometimes in this life we think we've gone too far in loving, but that's vanity. We've gone a lot further in being loved. The life to come is linked to this life, as loving is related to being loved. To love, that is really being satisfied with the image of a God who has gone a lot further in loving than in being loved.

A pastoral letter

One thing more. Evidently this song is an evensong. That doesn't mean the poet is in a romantic mood. Quite the contrary. He has reasons enough to be somber. What will morning bring? That's the way his doubt speaks. "I shall be satisfied with beholding thy form." That's the way his faith speaks.

While writing this we heard about the missile crisis in Cuba, and we were happy when morning came again. But there are and will be more crises. For the time being, ours remains an evening mood. Some day the big blow could come for me and for my world. The facts point to this, science points to this, and the Bible points to this.

But the Bible also points to something else. Were this not so it would make idols of facts and science. It can't let these have the last word. The Bible also knows about an unprecedented awakening.

"We cannot imagine that the worst will happen," said the 1962 *Pastoral Letter* of the Netherlands Reformed Church regarding armaments. "But, should that be the case, in the moment of annihilation may we be found to be men who refuse to hate and refuse to despair. If not in this rebellious province of the universe, then God will be love and light and life somewhere else. We know already that in this world each day can be our last and that a certain day will be our last. But on the other side of that day are resurrection and life."

Blessed hunger

An unprecedented awakening, provided it's in righteousness, the poet adds. After all, who will see God? Only the pure in heart. God grant us to die in righteousness when we die, and not on the side of violence or with a "fat heart." This language is dead serious. Happily, Jesus has added something. Happily, we also read, "Blessed are those who *hunger* and *thirst* for righteousness." These too will be satisfied (Matt. 5:6)!

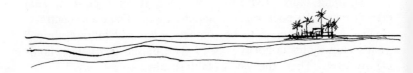

SOMETHING SPORTIVE

". . . by my God I can leap over a wall."

—Psalm 18:29

We're all familiar with the idea of a "wall." We think of that wall recently called a curtain, an iron curtain, a wall built right through Berlin as a symbol of enmity, terror, and challenge. We think also (we can't help but do so) of another wall without which the one just mentioned is unthinkable, a wall that was also a symbol of enmity, terror, and challenge—one that didn't divide Germans but divided Germans and all who were not Germans, all who were different and therefore inferior, especially the Jews. That's the wall we think of when we read John Hersey's book about the struggle of the Jewish ghetto in Warsaw, one of the most tragic books I know. He called it simply *The Wall,* from the enclosure within which Jews were chased like rats into sewers, even there to be smoked out and destroyed. Again, we think of the well-known wall against which so many Jews have leaned their heads, portraying a misery man cannot overcome—the Wailing Wall in Jerusalem. However, we don't have to look so far afield to realize that when anyone thinks of a wall as a wailing wall, he thinks of something that he sees as an insuperable wall, of things that are inexorable—so inexorable that he can dash himself against them as against a wall, to his hurt. Anyone who says "wall" speaks of pain, hardness, anxiety—all the way from the ordinary bump children get to that which the poet of our Psalm describes when he testifies: "The cords of death encompassed me."

Berlin in the Bible

That's the first thing we think of when we think of a wall. It's not just a word. It's the idea of a reality painfully familiar.

The second thing is that this is not only painfully familiar to us but is painfully familiar to the book we swear by and without which we can't get along—the Bible. That's one of the reasons why we swear by it and why we can't get along without it. The Bible is not unacquainted with our grief—let alone denies it. The walls we dread and by which we know ourselves captive run not only through Berlin. They run through the Bible. That should comfort us when we read this book.

Happy as a king

Of course, there's a difference. Contrasted with life in general the Bible not only lets us see the familiar wall—that would be poor comfort!—but it lets us see something else, someone else, God!

Let's avoid misunderstanding. To see God doesn't mean that we no longer have to see the wall, let alone that it should disappear! To speak of God in the Bible or in the life of a believer doesn't mean we no longer have to speak of walls. If we will read our text honestly and with open mind it's impossible to conclude that there are no walls any longer for the man with God. It means rather that we can get over the walls with God. That's a great difference!

It's such a great difference that in this Psalm we not only hear a man who feels himself prey to the waters of the netherworld, so hellish is his grief and so mortal his fear, but we discover that this same man knows he is "head of the nations." We don't have to say "chin up" to him! Apparently this is a Psalm of David, that David who was oppressed by Saul but who still knew he was called to become king in his place. Every believer, however, can apply this "somersault" to himself—indeed, he must if he is to feel happy as a king, with God.

The wall of life

Of course, this doesn't always happen at once. David's weal and woe which are pressed here into a single Psalm, took an enormous piece of his life. To be sure, walls can fall suddenly, not just in Jericho in some gray and improbable past, but also at a modern sickbed. Faith healers are not talking nonsense! But it can also take years to climb over the walls. For some it will take a lifetime and more. In a way, this whole life is something we have to climb over with God in order to land safely on a new earth, on the truly level ground of Psalm 143. It's not only death that takes lifelong training if we're to come through. All of life calls for it.

Something sportive

Still, there's something sportive about our text. I must not exaggerate this, lest the wall become harmless. Examined closely, the picture is certainly grim. Instead of reading "leap over a wall," we can with good reason read it with N. H. Ridderbos, "scale." It's certainly clear from the preceding verse that the wall spoken of is a fortified wall and not a bit of string stretched across a sport field. We're not leaping here for some mark or honor but for our very lives. Yet there's still something sportive in our text. It suggests a breathtaking swing. That's true for the whole of faith. It's like saying, "Quit fussing, boys. Jump!"

Let's not suppose something terribly important isn't involved. Adequate training! What won't a person do to make a good high jump! What will a person not give up for this? To speak of training is to speak of self-denial. Anyway, except for some jumpers, a high jump calls for a long dash. You don't make it theoretically but only in practice. It must be studied. It must be studied in life. That's called life experience. It must be studied in the Bible. That's called faith experience. Nor can we get along without a good trainer. Happily, One is available—One who doesn't talk casually about it as though He doesn't know what jumping or walls are. After all, "In all their affliction he was afflicted" (Isa.

63:9)! How? We see this best in Him who, according to the Epistle to the Hebrews, is our high priest, able "to sympathize with our weaknesses," and "who in every respect has been tempted as we are" (Heb. 4:14-15).

With such training we're able to make a tremendous leap. The poet was able to make the leap from deepest humiliation to kingship. No matter how greatly he had been tormented, he can apply to himself the image of "hinds' feet." What is lighter than that? A poet like Habakkuk does the same. When he was in the doldrums as seldom anyone has been, when as far as the eye can see he could only see a wall, he doesn't talk about the depths but about the heights. Like our poet he knows he is with God and feels like a hind (3:19).

How is that possible? Is it because with God he knows he is *out of the depths?* Or is it because he knows he is in the depths *with God?* Either way—with God it doesn't make any difference to him.

In the clear

There's something sportive about our Psalm. There's also something about politics in it. We don't have to be pacifists to realize that, to a large extent, the wall between East and West rests on misunderstanding. We don't have to be pacifists to know that we can't be satisfied with this but must somehow get over it and see more clearly than we see now. That's why something of sociology and theology must be included in it too, because these are also areas with whose walls we cannot be content. The really devilish thing about walls is that they aren't as high as they seem to be.

Besides all this, there's something eschatological in all this. There's the suggestion of a time when the walls of enmity, terror, and challenge will disappear, when death shall be no more, neither mourning nor crying nor pain—a time when we no longer have to go through doors because we'll have glorified bodies like Jesus (John 20:26). In our Psalm the foundations of all that makes this world so anxious are already trembling. When that happens in Matthew 28:2, an enormous wall of enmity is broken, the greatest and most virulent that ever was—the wall between God and man. In its fall another is dragged down with it—the separation between life and death. Thinking and dreaming and doing this, a man is already able to feel in the clear (Ps. 18:19).

The new Jerusalem

Finally, there's still something we've forgotten. Not only does the enemy have walls, not only does the devil devise them—God has them too. Fortunately! And these walls are such that no one can climb over them even if he wanted to.

The new Jerusalem, we read, has "a great, high wall" (Rev. 21:12). The same is implied in our Psalm, where we read that God is a "fortress" and a "rock."

Two things can and should be said about this wall. It's impregnable over against those who try to take it by force (vs. 42). Of course, for only within this wall is the mystery safe from the attack of others, and this mystery must be strongly guarded. Isn't that the "tree of life" (Gen. 3:22)?

That's not all. As forbidding as God's walls are for those who try to force them unlawfully, so open are they for those who do not try to seize the mystery but instead receive it. The great and high wall of the New Jerusalem has gates that "shall never be shut by day" (Rev. 21:25)! The city of God, the church, and the Christian—they are protection against disaster, but also a sally port for salvation.

The Lord God would not regard anything else as "something sportive"!

WHAT IS SWEETER THAN HONEY?

"... sweeter also than honey ..."

—Psalm 19:10

What is sweeter than honey? Put this way it sounds like a riddle from a fairy tale we heard or read when we were children—a riddle that the princess in the fairy tale puts to all who wish to win her. Whoever guesses it may marry her. Remember? Even if he's the poorest cobbler boy!

A fine marriage text

One could use the text very appropriately in celebrating a church wedding. After all, weddings have something of fairy tales about them, just as (to turn it around) in fairy tales there are often weddings.

To be sure, there's a difference. In a Christian wedding no princesses put riddles to those who must guess to win them. That means a Christian wedding isn't just a fairy tale. In a Christian wedding, riddles are not asked by princesses, or by a man and woman to each other. Instead, the Lord God puts one to husband and wife (Eph. 5:32)!

This difference makes the comparison richer, not poorer. The One who asks the riddle has more royal blood than all the princesses put together, and those who guess the riddle can be poorer than the poorest cobbler boy!

Bragging about it

But doesn't the Lord God make it harder for us with His riddles than the princesses in the fairy tales? Not at all. He manages to hide the answers in the questions and always gives the answer one way or another. The same is true here. What is sweeter than honey? The law!

I hope no one will be disappointed in this answer or think it's a rather sour answer to a sweet question. As if the Bible isn't aware that the answer might disappoint us! That's why the poet begins to brag about the law by comparing it with the sweetest things we know, telling us the law is always sweeter. He says the law is worth its weight in gold, quickly adding that it's worth more than gold, "even much fine gold." Another Psalm tells us that the law offers a wonderful view: ". . . thy commandment is exceeding broad" (Ps. 119:96). We could say, "broader than an ocean!" or again, we hear there's music in it (Ps. 119:54), and we could say, "Yes, and a lot more!" But we don't need to look anywhere else in the Bible. In our Psalm, the law is compared with creation—even with *the* creation as described magnificiently in the first seven verses. Again we could say, "Yes, and a lot more!" Look what those verses portray—a procession, a wedding, a feast—and a lot more!

He started it

Why is the law and the world of the law so marvelous and so much sweeter than honey? To speak of the law is to speak of the law of love. That's plain all through the Bible, even though it may be seen more clearly in some places than in others. Think, for example, of Romans 13:10, where we read that "love is the fulfilling of the law." The Bible simply doesn't know any other law than the law of love. There may be other laws, but they're not the laws of the Bible. They're the laws of pharisaism, and they're not sweeter than honey but bitter as gall. We should not listen to them.

What kind of love does the law of love describe? Love for one another, of course, but also love for God. Were that not so we would be able to make it too easy (or too hard) for one another. Doesn't God make it too hard for us? No. Who is the God we are to love? He's the God of whom it's written that He did not wait for us to love Him but began by loving us (1 John 4:10). On this basis I would say love never becomes bitter as gall but always remains sweeter than honey!

The riddle of love

We go back to where we began—to something very sweet—to the marriage of two persons for whom our text, as it were, is created.

What is sweeter than honey in marriage? To listen together to Mozart, or, if we're tired of that, to Sydney Bechet. To read a good book together, or to see a painting by Paul Klee. It doesn't have to be so sophisticated. To listen to Flip Wilson together, to have fun together, or, just to drink a cup of tea together and chat for an hour. All that is sweeter than honey.

But we haven't answered the riddle completely unless we add, to listen to God together. That means to listen to the law of love together. That means to see how His love penetrates all the crises of the world. That means to look to the cross, to go to Golgotha, and never see enough there. Always to be a bit absentminded, because our thoughts are there. What can be compared to that? That's sweeter than honey!

This riddle is too much for all of us. We simply can't say enough about it. We have to let it titillate our living. Our Psalm suggests that even the silent creation talks about it (vs. 4)—what else is the law of creation but the law of love? At its best, the latter catches up with the former in redemption. How much more than the silent creation should the most articulate creatures, people, talk about it! Our Psalm also suggests that nothing remains hidden from the glow of this law. Happily it also means that nothing remains hidden from the forgiveness of God's enormous love.

More difficult and more beautiful

That's how weddings can have something of the character of the fairy tale with which we begin. But more! Christian weddings undoubtedly are more difficult than those in fairy tales. But they're also more beautiful and certainly more real.

CHARIOTS AND HORSES

"Some boast of chariots, and some of horses;
but we will boast of the name of the Lord our God."

—Psalm 20:7

Was Israel pacifist? Was its exceptional place among the nations marked by this exception also, that it didn't fight as other peoples did, or that it fought differently—less violently and cruelly? The latter might be debatable but hardly the former. Israel was not pacifist.

A legitimate phenomenon

We have to admit that Israel was not unacquainted with pacifism, the voluntary laying down of weapons for one reason or other. It appeared as a legitimate phenomenon in the way Jeremiah confronted the king of Babylon. This has important consequences. It means, for example, that church history, which in this respect also is dependent on biblical history, has to recognize pacifism as a legitimate phenomenon. But such recognition of pacifism is hardly a rule. Nor is this contradicted by the fact that David is forbidden to build the temple because he had blood on his hands (1 Chron. 22:8). One can't conclude more from this narrative than that there may be *too* much blood on a person's hands, and that even in Israel the church must not always be dependent on the state. How much less now!

God not a rival

Our text doesn't *in itself* forbid a believer the use of "chariots and horses" or of various kinds of power (including force).

What then is forbidden in this text? Boasting about it is forbidden. That goes beyond "relying on." The latter is permissible and even obligatory—ranging all the way from a wife who is a "fit helper" (Gen. 2:18) to the sword of government which exists to drive a wedge between good and evil (Rom. 13:4). But trust in the all-encompassing sense of the word is trust in God. We may not trust anything or anyone in this way. That includes my wife as well. To do so would be idolatry, and then the Lord our God will become a "jealous" God (Exod. 20:5).

Such trust in God doesn't function as a rival of all else on which we rely. One of the most vehement summons to trust God in all the Bible—"Not by might, nor by power, but by my Spirit, says the LORD of hosts" (Zech. 4:6)—is uttered by the prophet within a city built with "trowel and sword" and with a wall so strong that "all the nations round about us were afraid and fell greatly in their own esteem" (Neh. 6:16). This doesn't alter the fact that these same nations have to acknowledge that "this work had been accomplished with the help of our God," or that the Israelite believed the *Lord* would be "a wall of fire" around him (Zech. 2:5).

The story of the temptation in the wilderness teaches us that trust in God can even have devilish origin (Luke 4:10-11), however it may appeal to such Bible texts as Psalm 91:11 ("For he will give his angels charge of you to guard you in all your ways. On their hands they will bear you up, lest you dash your foot against a stone"). In any case, it's quite evident that the king for whom this Psalm is written as a prayer stands on the eve of battle.

Of course, when it comes to the test we know better. Zechariah knew it too—that when the true King comes, He will not care about horses and chariots, and He will ride on a little donkey (Zech. 9:9). Paul knew it too. When he knew himself physically handicapped, at first (and quite legitimately) he sought relief from some ailment, but to no avail. Then he realized as never before that *the* power ultimately is made perfect in weakness (2 Cor. 12:9).

But one may not conclude from the foregoing that use of "chariots and horses" or other kinds of force to ward off trouble or assist a man or a nation is *in itself* evil.

Watch out

Meantime, let's watch out. Sunday 34 of the Heidelberg Catechism is especially relevant to the situation described in our text. It defines idolatry: "to imagine or possess something in which to put one's trust in place of or beside the one true God who has revealed himself in his Word"—not only "in place of" but also "beside." Doubtless no believer deliberately looks for something or someone to give himself to completely in place of God. That's not where the danger lies. According to our text not even the pagan adversaries can be accused of this. If for Israel trust in God didn't exclude use of "horses and chariots," neither for pagans did horses and chariots exclude trust in a god. But their god was only an idol and must be written with a small "g," because even if trust in him doesn't wholly vanish into trust in "horses and chariots," at least it gives way to the latter. That's what we must watch out for —that relying on other securities, not objectionable in themselves, does not assume such importance that there will no longer be any real place for God beside them—so that at best there would only be room for an idol. In the long run it remains true that "No man can serve two masters: for . . . he will hate the one and love the other" (Matt. 6:24, K.J.V.). What is intended to be "beside" Him sooner or later comes to be "in place of" Him.

How afraid the Bible is that our trust in all sorts of securities beside God will become too great is often seen in those battles won with a minimum of weaponry but with a maximum of trust in God. Think of the story of Gideon or of David's sling against Goliath's sword. Once it even happened that people were able to win without any weapons at all. Think of the conquest of Jericho by singing, which is to say, by trust in God. We may not draw from this a rule for every kind of conflict in every age, but we should be warned by such examples. It should also be noted that kings of Israel only reluctantly began to seek "many horses." It should also be noted that when Israel pits all its available material strength against the enemy, time and again this is viewed with reservations (Ps. 33:17; cf. Ps. 147:10; Isa. 31:3; Mic. 5:9).

Polaris submarines and hydrogen bombs

All this is warning for us in a time when we're no longer concerned with "horses and chariots," or even with "tanks and cannon," but with "polaris submarines and hydrogen bombs." In an issue of *Church and Peace,* of the association of Christian Pacifists of Holland, I noticed a cartoon in which the political leaders who then were calling the tune were all kneeling before the idol of the atom bomb. That determined all they did and did not do. All of them were there—not only Khrushchev but Macmillan, de Gaulle, and Kennedy. Not only godless bolshevists but also Christian statesmen! The cartoon was a bit unfair, I think, but I do believe we should heed it. Dr. Boerwinkel is quite right when he said that our greatest danger is not the atom bomb but trust in the atom bomb. Let's heed the warning. If all this was true for a time when the worst weapons were "chariots and horses," how much more is it true when we're dealing with materials much more serious and perhaps idolatrous and for that reason annihilating. Today it's no longer "chariots and horses." We ought to think a hundred times before we think of wars as "wars of the Lord."

We'd better do "everything" to guard against one more war breaking out. I'm sure pacifists and non-pacifists agree on this. Where they disagree and dispute is whether this "everything" we must do to prevent war means we must lay down all arms as our expression of trust in God, or whether we can rely on threat of arms and still trust in God. Each side has to wrestle with the question whether its own position might possibly be a devilish temptation instead of "the command of this hour." Both sides must respect each other in this wrestling instead of jeering each other.

TOTAL WAR

"The Lord will swallow them up in his wrath . . ."

—Psalm 21:9

If in Psalm 20 we stand before a victory, in Psalm 21 victory has been won. (The new translation of the Netherland Bible Society suggests this in its superscriptions, and there's no reason to question this.) This Psalm, like the preceding one, is a war Psalm —a very grim war Psalm. That's evident in such phrases as "you will aim at their faces with your bows." (In the Dutch translation, as in the King James Version, this "you" is God.) What we read about the consequences of this war bears this out strongly. "You will destroy their offspring from the earth." Not only their off-spring, but their descendants, will be destroyed from among "the sons of men." Here there's no limiting to the third and fourth generation (Exod. 20:5). It suggests the kind of war we have begun to call "total war," the worst possible.

The third world war?

To be sure, it didn't actually happen like this. Perhaps it did in the consciousness of those involved, whether friend or foe. That says a great deal. If my world crumbles, the whole world crumbles; if my world celebrates victory, the whole world celebrates. Nonetheless, it didn't happen as totally as here described.

Actually there's only one situation known to us in which a war could break out as grim and total as here suggested. Then we could speak of a "blazing oven" everywhere, and destruction could strike everyone in such a way that all descendants would be included without exception. That's modern war—not even the two modern wars behind us, but the dread third war that never ceases to terrify us. Only this third war could bring the grim climate of our Psalm to full expression.

Three questions

But there are differences or at least question marks which break the analogy and keep us from deducing this third war out of our Psalm.

First of all, our Psalm makes it plain that the power is God's power. That's beyond dispute. It's evident not only because the Psalm closes with "We will sing and praise thy power," but because the whole Psalm is characterized by the way in which the "I" retreats before the "Thou." The king, the head of his own side, doesn't rejoice in his own power. His blessings, his crown, his life, his whole position, everything on which his own power and honor stands or falls—it all stands or falls with the power and honor and prestige of his God. That's why it's hard for either side today to feel at home in the atmosphere of this Psalm. One side is indifferent to it, since communism is atheism. But it's debatable whether the other side, the "Christian" side, can be at home in it. We can hardly say that the power of the West can be called the power "of the Lord." Our side isn't raising a true song of praise as the proper conclusion to all we have to say, as in the case of this Psalm.

Secondly, after raising a question about the West, we must also raise one about the East in connection with the God-haters we meet in the Psalm. Can we say that the East excels in hatred of God? If we grant this, don't we have to ask which God is hated in the East? Is it the God of Israel? Or is it an image that the West has made of the God of Israel? To what extent does the image still look like Him?

A third question. In our Psalm—rather, in the battle described in the Psalm—some survive and some perish. That's not unusual because so far it's been true of every war. What is unusual about total war as we fear it, however, is that there won't be any survivors on either side.

Eschatological

This last difference reminds us that the climate of the Psalm doesn't fit our time, or any time. If today there would be no survivors on either side, whereas there used to be survivors on both sides, our Psalm portrays a situation in which there are survivors on only one side. That's strange.

As we've mentioned earlier and as Van Ruler has reminded us, we have to read the Old Testament eschatologically—that is, as portraying conditions that will only be wholly true for the last day and for the last judgment. I emphasize this because we have no right to say the kinds of dread situations portrayed as the outbreak of God's wrath will not happen. Even of these, however, we have to say that they stand for a "more" and a "later." The Old Testament is not out of date, nor is the passionate ethic of our Psalm, for even in the New Testament we hear "It is a fearful thing to fall into the hands of the living God" (Heb. 10:31), and "our God is a consuming fire" (Heb. 12:29). This the "oven" of our Psalm illustrates with glorious gentleness as well as with frightening severity. Only then will some things in our Psalm which are not only diagnosed but desired become fully clear. There's always something left for which Israel hopes! But total war, as we can or try to understand it, could only be an imitation of this, a caricature—if only because it won't be followed by the total peace to which this Psalm points us.

The church

If only for a moment we must let go of thoughts about our wars and our sides, and fall back on the one thing that matters for total survival, because "the gates of Hades shall not prevail against it" (i.e., the church) (Matt: 16:18). Men from East and

West still flee to the church to "praise God's power with Psalms."
The church knows that total judgment belongs to God.

Luther was right in observing that this Psalm "contains a prophecy of the Kingdom of Christ (= church). The Jews understand this psalm simply of a king as though it were an epode sung after the preceding psalms. But it seems too strong for that to me. I mean, we must understand it in terms of the resurrected and glorified Christ. Since Christ now reigns it is a right cheerful psalm."

FORSAKEN BY GOD

"My God, my God, why hast thou forsaken me?"

—Psalm 22:1

The Psalmist is in distress—and what distress! His distress approaches what we call (supposing it a modern idea) the absence of God. It approaches André Schwarz-Bart's *The Last of the Just* and John Hersey's *The Wall,* books in which the Jewish "worm" (vs. 6) of our Psalm sees himself encircled and crushed by modern "bulls of Bashan." When we read these books which are not only about death pits but are themselves a great pit we can see how God-forsaken is that pit. The distress of this Jew approximates the distress of his fellow Jews as we "accompanied" them during 1940-1945. To put it more strongly, this distress covers the other in the double sense of the word, as atrocious as it is comforting.

Head and heart

Jesus Christ has made this distress and this Psalm His own in the very depths of His existence, on the cross. He literally made it His own. We meet the phrase "All who see me mock at me" in Matthew 27:39. The mocking "He committed his cause to the LORD; let him deliver him, let him rescue him, for he delights in him" is found in Matthew 27:43. The phrase "they divide my garments among them, and for my raiment they cast lots" is found in John 19:24. The climax of the misery which we meet here, "My God, my God, why hast thou forsaken me?" is found in Matthew 27:46. There are further analogies. "I will tell of thy name to my brethren; in the midst of the congregation I will praise thee"—this we can also read in Hebrews 2:11-12. But there we're really beyond the brink of the distress and no longer at the cross. That comes later.

Because Jesus Christ literally quotes Psalm 22:1, some have understood this as a bit of liturgy. If we don't let this weaken the solidarity described above, there's no reason to object. But is it necessary? After all, others have appealed to the Bible and especially to the Psalms in their struggle with death. Herman Bavinck [1] did this quite literally on his deathbed. Who would dare question that Jesus knew His Bible in head and heart? What else does this mean if not that He knew our distress, our forsakenness, in head and heart?

Man: a question mark

That was hell for Him. The Heidelberg Catechism for Sunday 16 says it was *the* hell for Him. Something became a question mark for Him—even for Him! Even He had not realized that becoming man could be so bad, that so much is bound up with becoming man, a loneliness that can be called God-forsakenness.

Does this mean a question mark is placed after God? Doesn't it say this? In the deepest sense, no. In the deepest sense, it's a question mark placed after man—indeed, it is *the* question mark placed after man. As Lamentations 3:39 puts it in different words, the depth of sorrow is guilt—and that says something! In other words, God may be a problem for man, but He can never be the greatest problem. That's man before God. How terrible and comforting is this. It took three days before a full answer came.

---

1. TRANSLATOR'S NOTE: Herman Bavinck (before Gerrit Berkouwer) was the best-known theologian of the author's denomination. His most important work is the four-volume *Gereformeerde Dogmatiek*, 1906-1911.

Imagination

For us it doesn't have to come in this way because we have this behind us. From now on we know and will always know that with Jesus there is deliverance from this barren God-forsakenness. Thanks to Him we've come to know this so well that even the word has become a bit unreal to us. Is there actually something like being forsaken by God? When we feel forsaken by God—and it does happen—isn't God bringing us in the vicinity of that utter dereliction at the cross—near but no closer—so that we realize with a shock that we've been *imagining* something? Of course, no one has the right to tell another he's imagining this. But doesn't Jesus have the right? Did anyone ever take my distress upon himself as He did?

The poet is a prophet

One gets the impression that the poet had some idea about these things. According to N. H. Ridderbos, it's possible that he penned his song of thanksgiving (which begins in verse 22) after his deliverance and that both songs are brought together at the feast of the thank offering. According to the same writer, however, it's also possible that the poet "immediately added the thanksgiving to the lament in the certainty of being heard." The latter possibility is the more interesting for faith and is certainly possible! There's even room for Luther's words about this verse: "Already he prophesies the resurrection as if it were already granted."

To the end

Under such perspectives a man begins to feel very small, "meek" (vs. 26, K.J.V.), if he had not already. His great distress becomes smaller through all this, if it were not already. He can't stop telling it everywhere, to shout it "upon the housetops" (Matt. 10:27).

Of course, he will first tell it to his "brethren." They will be the happiest to hear it. Could it be they need it most because they were not equal to the doubt? But he will not stop there. The happiness attained in our Psalm reaches out not only to brothers and sisters but even to "the ends of the earth." Mission and evangelism come into view. The same Ridderbos says we should note "that in this powerful messianic Psalm there is no prayer for vengeance whereas the prospect is held out that even the Gentiles will turn to the Lord." Even their "descendants" are mentioned. That is to say, deliverance from distress will accompany us not only to the end of the earth but also to the end of the age. That may have something to say to those situations in which we sigh that "the end is not yet." Our Psalm leads us to Matthew 28:20: "and lo, I am with you always, to the close of the age."

A wonderful expression

If the Jew already had some idea of this, surely the Christian has. Of what precisely? That the world is filled with the God-forsakenness of Jesus Christ. That's a wonderful expression.

This is so because after the "My God, my God, why hast thou forsaken me?" we hear Him say with a loud voice, "It is finished!" Since that time the world is filled with the God-forsakenness of Jesus Christ—filled with shame and with comfort. The world is so full of the God-forsakenness of Jesus Christ that there really isn't any place left for our own.

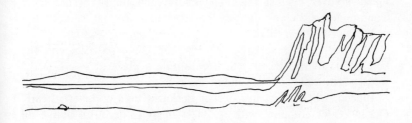

THE PICNIC OF THE GOSPEL

*"Thou preparest a table before me
in the presence of my enemies."*

—Psalm 23:5

I'm not sure about others, but I know that church people tend to think of this table and this distress not just as any table or any distress. They are likely to think of a very particular table and of a very special distress, the greatest possible. That isn't the anxiety of newspaper, radio, or "others" in the world outside. After all, it's not what "goes into the mouth"—what happens to a man— but what "comes out of the mouth" that defiles a man (Matt. 15:17-18). In saying this Jesus means the heart, not the outer but the inner world of man, and the greatest anxiety that dwells there from the beginning. He means sin, my sin.

The worst and the best

If sin is the special anxiety for a churchman, what is the special table set over against this? The churchman thinks of the Holy Communion. Catching sight of this from time to time, he sees that in the midst of sin there is a place of forgiveness, a morsel of release, a cup of deliverance. It's like the green pastures and the still waters of this Psalm which constitute a place of safety in the midst of the valley of the shadow of death.

Indeed, what valley has deeper darkness than a sinner's heart? Oceans can't compare with it. "The heart is deceitful above all things, and desperately corrupt; who can understand it?" (Jer. 17:9). And what is more grassy, refreshing, lovelier, more re-creative than to go with such a heart to the Lord's Supper? No spring can compare with this. And who is more hospitable than a Host who gives Himself as our well-known Savior of the world, who applies this Psalm to Himself (John 10:1-16)?

Isn't it so? We think immediately of the familiar table called the Communion table in the midst of the familiar anxiety called sin. To ignore this and to run toward anxieties "dearer" to us would mean that we're Pharisees. The poet felt this. That's why he dares to talk about a leading "in paths of righteousness," a leading from the worst to the best.

Going out with God

But when, thanks to this Supper, our greatest and most worri-some anxiety of sin is solved, we haven't escaped our other anxi-eties—those of newspaper, of radio, "the others," the outside world. The world of the Psalms is full of these anxieties. We read of plague and arrows, of lion and adder. Such language is not out of date. We still meet lions and bears on the road, and there are still snakes in the grass all around us. The arrow of temptation still strikes today, and there are still things I royally detest—the anxi-eties of newspapers, radio, "the others," the world outside.

Fortunately, in the midst of all this is also the image of the ta-ble. Here the image is not simply that of the forgiveness of sins (unless this forgiveness now refers to the "others"). Now the im-age of the table is that of protection, of rest and safety, of fellow-ship in the midst of a time that's terrible in many respects. It's the image of a God who says, "Son, shall we have a bite together? You need to get away awhile!" Indeed, the image is one of getting away awhile—with God.

There's something provocative and impertinent about this, some-thing tremendously reassuring, over against the language of news-paper and radio—something like green pastures and still waters. In the midst of the valley of the world there is a comradeship with God, a quite simple comradeship with God.

Every meal a communion

It's not only at the Lord's Supper that all this comes to mind
and takes us by surprise. It should take us by surprise at every
meal. It should take us by surprise anywhere and anytime in the
traffic of our daily life. God will see to it that life has some relish
in the midst of all the many anxieties that are no less part of daily
life.

Speaking of anxieties, this makes us think of a very familiar
biblical narrative. I'm thinking of the story of Paul in the storm
—especially of what he did when the storm reached its height,
and when men had already thrown overboard not only precious
cargo but even the ship's rigging, in the hope they might save
themselves by doing so. We read he "took bread, and giving
thanks to God in the presence of all he broke it and began to eat"
(Acts 27:35). There you have it again! In the midst of the valley
of the shadow of death, a table is set again, the table of Psalm 23.
Evidently Paul kept his appetite for life; he didn't give up!

The picnic of the gospel

That still doesn't say everything. Something else is said about
that meal of Paul—rain or shine! We read: "Then they all were
encouraged and ate some food themselves" (Acts 27:36). In
the midst of circumstances not especially Christian, it was a Christian's behavior that did it, that made the difference!

That's really tremendous. That doesn't lie. When in the midst
of all sorts of present anxieties, we partake of the Lord's Supper
or, for that matter partake of any nourishment in this way, that
doesn't lie. Then is seen a morsel of trust in God in the midst of
the world, like a meadow in a jungle of sin and like a pond in the
ocean of daily news. The poet of Psalm 23 tells us that in the
midst of everything wild and waste there is the intimate, simple,
joyous, daring, needed, and fascinating picnic of the gospel.

SANCTIFICATION AND CULTURE

"Lift up your heads, O gates!
and be lifted up, O ancient doors!
that the King of glory may come in."

—Psalm 24:7

In this Psalm we hear the same note struck as in Psalm 15. That is to say, this sound is not for everyone. On the basis also of this Psalm we must say that not everybody can go to church. Another way of saying this is that not every church is really a church. There are false churches. I'm not thinking now of the way we usually understand this—lack of discipline or false doctrine— though I certainly want to hold to the standards of the Netherland Confession of Faith. But I'm thinking of what this Psalm understands as lack of discipline or as false teaching—namely, not to have clean hands and a pure heart, to seek perfidy and to pledge fidelity to a wrong cause. A church can be involved in society and in politics in a false way. This can even assume such proportions that Bonhoeffer asked the ecumenical church of his day to exercise discipline over his own German church, and not without reason. And it's by no means evident why a fascist situation is the only one in which a church would stand under the standard of Psalms like Psalm 24.

The King of glory

Nor is the only note which our Psalm has in common with Psalm 15 the same strong ethic. When we examined the promise of steadfastness with which Psalm 15 ends, we took this to mean preservation not only in the precarious-in-general but in the ethical-in-particular. In other words, man's sanctification in Psalm 15 is not at the expense of God's justification. We reach the same conclusion here. What the man of Psalm 24 has to offer his fellow-man doesn't mean he himself is any less dependent upon God.

This is evident in various ways. To begin, take the phrase "the LORD's" in verse 1. If verse 4, with all its rich content, belongs to the "fulness" of the earth (and it's certainly not an afterthought), then we observe at once whereon this foundation—not only of "The earth . . . and the fulness thereof, the world and those who dwell therein," but also of the sanctification described—rests. The clue is the subject "he" (verse 2). One would be an out-and-out moralist to want to separate the moral demand of verse 4 from the blessing, vindication, and salvation given in verse 5. Especially striking is the word "seek" in verse 6, since it comes from the lips of those who have so much to offer! We could apply the word of Jesus to the content of verse 4: "seek, and you will find" (Matt. 7:7). We should not forget the interpretation Professor Brillenburg Wurth once gave in a *Horizon* article—namely, that it could be that only those who keep seeking keep finding.

The most moving note is still to come. At the end of the Psalm someone is brought into the picture. Who? Is it the man who knows he has kept verse 4? Suddenly he seems to be left behind as an "unprofitable servant," the unprofitable servant Jesus said we all are when we have done all we could do (Luke 17:10, K.J.V.). When it comes to the test, who receives honor? Not I, not man-in-general, not even kings-in-general (even if they are wise and come from the East, Matt. 2:1). There's only one "King of glory" (vs. 7).

Why do we think especially of Jesus Christ when we think of this king? Not least because He fulfilled verse 4 in the most extraordinary way, understanding by "clean hands" the nails in His hands, and by "pure heart" the knowledge that Satan could not separate Him from us in the wilderness, and by "not swearing deceitfully" remaining true to us even to death—and what a death!

Nothing is to prevent us from following this King. We'd better follow Him (Matt. 10:38)! That means two things. It means something glorious, for it means that He wants us to follow Him when He goes through the gates. I once heard Professor Berkouwer say that one of the greatest words in the Bible is the word in which Jesus promises us a glory which, nota bene, was *His* (John 17:22)! But that also means something painful. After all, the "servant is not greater than his master" (John 13:16). These gates, no matter how large—and they're never large enough, for they can't lift up their heads high enough (vs. 7)—can't begin small enough (Matt. 7:13). The way to verses 7-8 begins in verse 4.

Sanctification and culture

It's tempting not to leave the Psalm yet. It's tempting not only to seek its meaning in sanctification but also to seek its meaning for culture, which was the same thing for a man like Kuyper. If verse 4 brings us especially to the former (sanctification), verse 1, "The earth . . . and the fulness thereof," brings us to the latter (culture). We can't let go of this thought when we think of the gates and their "ancient doors."

As with sanctification, culture also can make us anxious. To grasp one, as to grasp the other, is an enormous grasp. Both seem to lie as far from us and so far beyond our grasp—culture perhaps even more seriously so than sanctification. But we can't leave it there. The Psalm not only wants to make "inward dwellings in our hearts"; it also wants to make "other, actual dwellings in things" (Noordmans). How the world of culture can make us anxious! How are we to come into it and through it? How narrow the way can be to a conception of culture! How much can haunt us before the "heads" are "lifted up" (vs. 7)! How we can suffocate in the "fulness" of verse 1! We can link this with what N. H. Ridderbos observes about the gates mentioned in this Psalm. "We recall that once Jerusalem, and possibly the citadel of Zion had been the sacral place of another deity." The phrase "the LORD's" of verse 1 will have to help us, and that's the way Kuyper links culture with sanctification. Culture must be set free from idolatry, must be demythologized and brought to pure insight and outlook.

Meanwhile, that involves quite a struggle. Once these things were paradisically simple, but we cannot go back to that "pre-history." For that matter, we'd have to throw culture away if we tried, for when we speak of paradise we speak more of nature than of culture. We have to go forward. One day "the glory and the honor of the nations" will be wholly subject to Him (Rev. 21:26). One day everything will be safe. But how will it be in the meantime, and how do we get to that day?

The poet Coert Poort gives an answer in his beautiful adaptation of this Psalm—a first-rate Advent hymn—in the words:

> The earth is the Lord's!
>   who shall tread on her
>   who shall go over the plains
>   without being afraid
>   who shall stand in the heart
>   of the primal forest
>   without fear
>   who shall walk through cities
>   without unrest
>   who shall sit at the window
>   without vexation?
> He has founded it on the seas
> and established it on the waters:
>   we live in unsteady places
>   our houses stand at the street corners
>   they stand in the weather as though born blind
>   we think of tomorrow
>   who shall go up the streets in the night
>   who shall find the door in the dark
>   who shall rest in peace?
> Open your hands and wait, wait patiently
> keep yourself ready at the window
> make your houses transparent

open your eyes and see
expectation already stretches itself as a bow
over the street
Now slowly your King draws near
He rides toward the crown of His names.

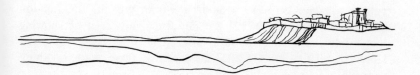

YOUTHFUL FOLLY

"Remember not the sins of my youth . . ."

—Psalm 25:7

Is youth as bad as it has been painted? We're inclined to think so because of all the "stories" we've heard. I put this in quotation marks, but we're still inclined to believe it because of these "stories" quite a bit *is* true! It's well to keep the quotation marks because not a few of these stories have been exploited by the yellow press. Despite our indignation over such articles as the well-known *Spiegel* series, however, we can't respond by pretending there's nothing to it.

A pastoral letter

I like what a "pastoral letter" of the Gereformeerde Classis The Hague said about this because it didn't exaggerate. Of course, we can relativize everything by showing that there has always been a playboy-type, weak if not malicious. Krantz and Vercruyse, the authors of the study *Youth in Question,* have shown convincingly (over against Professor J. H. van den Berg) that this sort of convulsive behavior isn't just a modern way of growing up. London had trouble with it in 1712! We can also relativize it by showing that adults have their failings, and we'll come to that shortly. However, all this doesn't alter the fact that there is such a thing as youthful folly.

I'm not thinking primarily of a particular type that hangs around the drugstore, etc. I simply mean that youth has its weaknesses, its particular sins, and its special temptations that it often "kicks wide open." Again, I don't think that the expression "youthful folly" suggests there are certain people who, unhappily enough, have something like this behind them. It suggests *everyone* has something like this behind him and could talk about it—about things he "used to do." This not only includes mischief but things about which he'd rather not talk at all—even if it's not necessarily whores and booze, the things Luther saw youth heading for in his day. (Read what Calvin has to say about this!)

Our text doesn't intend to suggest that David's youth happened to be *so* bad. We don't know anything about that—in contrast to what he did at a later age! The text does suggest David was firmly convinced that when young you have to watch out for very special dangers that are connected with being young, and that, alas, watching out for these doesn't always help.

Human shortcoming

This means that we don't do boys and girls a favor by trusting them in everything and by letting them do anything, simply because they're still young and look so innocent.

If we're inclined to do this it will be more under the influence of Rousseau (even if we've never read him) than of the Bible. We may appeal now and then to a Bible text—like the one where Jesus says we must "become like children" (Matt. 18:3), trying to infer from this that children are better than adults because they're more innocent and naïve. Quite apart from the fact that we must not think of the little lad whom Jesus had before him when we speak of youthful folly, his words don't in any way point us to "advantages" a child may have, but rather to "disadvantages."

After all, a child is the very picture of human shortcoming. He can't reach everything yet. He still has to be helped in everything, for he's the picture of dependence. Jesus' word holds the remembrance of our shortcomings and is a summons to dare confess

them before God. Parents can't appeal to this text when they want
their children to make a good impression as long as possible. At
the most they can appeal to it when they confess that they themselves, with their shortcomings, may be the reason their children
make a bad impression.

A rose of youth

On the other hand, older people must never use a text like ours
to start worrying their children (which is the opposite of patting
them on the back). After all, the Bible says youth is a wonderful
time and that we ought to get out of it all that's in it (Eccles.
11:9). We ought to keep sorrow from the heart and disease from
the body as long as we can. In other words, we ought to stay
young. We ought to cling to the world of sports and play and
good looks and sexuality and health as long as we can! According
to the Bible, parents ought to encourage all this instead of putting
it down. Yet it's no accident that in the midst of all this vital and
impetuous language of Ecclesiastes there is a warning: "But know
that for all these things God will bring you into judgment." Nor is
it an accident that the Psalmist has to face the question "How can
a young man keep his way pure?" (Ps. 119:9). Even Job, so sure
he could not have done anything wrong in the past but apparently
must have done so, thinks God is making him do penance for the
"iniquities of my youth" (Job 13:26).

But older people have no business worrying the younger on this
account. If they want to follow the leading of our Psalm, they
won't try to gloss over shortcomings (that's impossible), but they
will not worry their children. Youth has worries enough. Parents
should learn to forgive. That's what parents are for! And they
ought to do this because of Him who especially in this respect
wants to be older than all of us so that His grace may always be
older than our sin. We hear the poet say this when he pleads: "Be
mindful of thy mercy, O LORD, and of thy steadfast love, for they
have been from of old."

When that happens, man's memory of youth is like Israel's
memory of the wilderness—a time of complaining and murmur-

ing, rebellion and unbelief, but especially the memory of a God
who even then made the desert blossom like a rose in a hundred
and one ways.

The notable years

Now it's time for adults to get their turn. In his commentary on
our text, N. H. Ridderbos remarks: "besides the sins of his youth
the poet mentions his transgressions, letting us know that the man
of riper years sins more willingly and knowingly. That is why his
sin bears a more serious character."

It's typical of adults that they immediately took the pastoral letter mentioned above as striking at youthful folly without even noticing that the letter took care not to direct itself only to youth.
For many adults it's simply obvious that "youth has done it
again!"

We really ought to let these young people prepare a pastoral
letter about adults, about their parents. That might frighten the
congregation more than is now the case. Youth may have its own
particular shortcomings—no one denies this—but so have adults.
If youth breaks the fifth commandment, adults do the same with
the seventh commandment—and we don't have to limit adultery
to sexual misconduct. Boredom is sufficient and looks dark enough
—would it were black enough instead of appearing "gray." This is
true of more than the seventh commandment.

Adults are not sufficiently aware of this. They have their youthful follies behind them—the time they broke windows, or had love
affairs about which fortunately only two people knew. Now
they've become "pious and upright," or "virtuous and decent"—as
we could translate verse 21. That's the way they're known. That's
the way they feel protected, covered, settled. If only it were so! If
only they really would *let* themselves be protected instead of
trying to be protectors of their own piety and uprightness! If only
they would read carefully! If only they had ears to hear! Then
they would see that something stands behind verse 21 which at
first sight seems to contradict it. Reading only the first half of
verse 21, a person might be tempted to think, "Now I've arrived.

I'm in—thanks to my virtue and decency." Many people think this way. But the sentence isn't finished—"for I wait for thee." Actually the first half means nothing without the second. All our neat, tidy, and settled middle age, those notable years, mean nothing unless we base them on our hope in God and keep them based there instead of on ourselves.

The proper blush

Maybe young people are a bit less respectable (literally: obedient, less easily committed, and docile) and less virtuous (literally: unresponsive to obligations) than adults are. That's perfectly possible, and it's not good. These concepts don't belong to nineteenth-century morality as much as youth likes to think. They have characterized the church in all ages, even if we must not demand too much: "Youth is simply not yet prepared for virtue, the blood is still too young and too strong to control itself" (Luther). On the other hand, can't adults learn something from youth's expectancy? We think of this when we see the expectancy of hungry sparrows in their nest, or a young soldier on duty, or an athlete in his jump, or a proper blush, or a pregnancy.

Conclusion

Let's not argue about this any longer. Youth and adults can keep on worrying each other, and they ought to stop. Our Psalm concludes: "Redeem Israel, O God, out of all his troubles."

Israel includes all people. We ought to recall Malachi 4:6 ("And he will turn the hearts of fathers to their children and the hearts of children to their fathers . . ."), and we ought to recall Matthew 1:21 (". . . he will save his people from their sins").

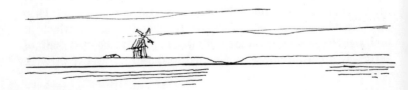

I WASH MY HANDS IN INNOCENCE

"I wash my hands in innocence . . ."

—Psalm 26:6

In this Psalm someone washes his hands in innocence. Let's hope that's true not only in this Psalm! Surely the intent is that every believer in time will be able to say with the poet that he has "walked in my integrity" and similar expressions, including the vigorous "But as for me" we meet in the third protestation of innocence in verse 11. Being faithful requires a certain distance, a separation, a break—else, according to our Psalm, it becomes unfaithfulness, the rankest kind of godlessness, atheism.

A parable repealed

More than any other, this Psalm has made the impression of pharisaism to many commentators. Yet it's precisely this kind of Psalm that can keep us from two things. In the first place, it can keep us from becoming Pharisees. In the second place, it can keep us from doing the opposite, mistaking ourselves for the tax collector in Jesus' parable. In our Psalm the parable of the Pharisee and the tax collector (Luke 18:9-14) is repealed, so to speak.

Around the altar

We had better begin with the former. This Psalm doesn't create Pharisees. Its guarantees are too many and too strong for that.

After the confident introduction, "Vindicate me, O LORD, for I have walked in my integrity," we discover that this expression doesn't exclude but rather includes another expression, as humble as the former is confident. "I have trusted in the LORD"! In verse 2, the Psalmist not only says that he "isn't half bad" ("Prove me, O LORD, and try me; test my heart and my mind"), but provides a particular explanation ("For")—"thy steadfast love is before my eyes"! In verse 11 we meet a separation ("But as for me . . .") that seems to savor of pharisaism in all its glory, but we can dismiss that glory because it is followed immediately by a confession of insignificance ("redeem me, and be gracious to me"). All this isn't so different from Peter's confession: "Lord, you know everything; you know that I love you"—a confession which in turn includes the commission "Feed my sheep" (John 21:17).

In an article in *Horizon*, Professor Koole pointed out that all such protestations of innocence (which are not confined to this Psalm, as we saw when studying Psalms 1, 7, 15, 24) have an altar in their midst. In other words, they revolve around God's grace which induced them.

Something good

That altar and the central place of grace make us think of the altar of redemption and of the grace of forgiveness. Much in our lives doesn't warrant a profession of innocence but rather the opposite, for much needs to be and happily can be redeemed. We recall Psalm 19:12: "But who can discern his errors? Clear thou me from hidden faults."

However, it's not enough to think of that. We have to think of something more. This altar is bathed with songs of thanksgiving as well as with professions of innocence. These songs of thanksgiving are not only thanksgivings for the forgiveness of what was wrong. We should not always make that primary, even in church, lest we twist the parable of the Pharisee and the tax collector in the direction of the latter. Songs of thanksgiving are also thanksgiving for the grace that *there is something good*.

Grace and good works

Of course, this too is a matter of grace. The song of praise is not offered to the poet himself but to his God. There is no place here for merit. Nor, for that matter, is there in Jesus' introduction to the Sermon on the Mount when he says we are the salt of the earth and the light of the world—which is to say that we are to exist on good works which he enumerates explicitly. He adds no less explicitly that these are not to be limited to the heart but must be seen publicly. They must be seen by men.

Someone may think this comes close to pharisaism. However, when we are close to Jesus this is impossible. That's clear from the little phrase in which Jesus says he not only wants men to see our good works, but he wants (indeed, he wills) them *so that* "they may . . . give glory to your Father who is in heaven" (Matt. 5:13-16).

Not only the forgiveness of our worst but the presence of our good works is a matter of grace. To turn it around, this grace is a matter of good works. The "For" in our Psalm shows the good works from the grace (verse 3) as well as the grace from the good works (verse 1).

Pontius Pilate

Someone else once said what the poet says here: "I wash my hands in innocence." However, he said this under circumstances that have made the expression pejorative rather than loved—"by Pontius Pilate" instead of "from Psalm 26." In other words, the expression has become a bit contaminated.

Pontius Pilate must have thought something along these lines: "I've got to crucify Jesus Christ. I really don't want to, but I can't help it. It goes against my grain, but there's nothing I can do. I wash my hands in innocence" (Matt. 27:24).

We had better watch out lest we find ourselves in the same situation. It goes against our grain too. We have less against Jesus Christ and what he demands than Pilate had. After all, he was a pagan and we're Christians. We know full well what the Christian way is and what we ought to do in this or that situation. But it still goes against our grain and, before we know it, something has gone wrong and ended wickedly. But we wash our hands in innocence. We really couldn't help it that what should have been didn't come from our hands, let alone Psalm 26!

A person who tries to say this forgets that Psalm 26 is not only the maximum but also the minimum (which is the same in the Kingdom of heaven). He forgets that the profession of innocence in this Psalm isn't made before something important happens. It doesn't assume that nothing of this sort has occurred but comes only after that something has happened.

Soiled hands and clean hands

This is an important Psalm. It tells us that we need to wash our hands, and that we can't wash our hands in innocence in the wrong way. Not to do it the right way is to do it the wrong way —and the latter had a good deal to do with the crucifixion of Jesus Christ. That's one side of it. From it we can learn how not to get soiled hands, at least not too soiled. But from it we can also learn how to get clean hands. We can learn how a man can be saved. We can stake the needed assurance of salvation on it. We can learn how, at the last day, we will dare say, "I have walked in my integrity."

That's possible if we not only *say* it, if *we* not only say it, if it's *apparent*, even as the poet sings his praise "aloud" (vs. 7). In other words, it's the others who need to be convinced of my innocence. Woe is me if I'm the only one convinced of this! We recall what the Heidelberg Catechism, Sunday 32, has to say about this when speaking of good works. We ought to do good works for various reasons. One of these is "so that we ourselves may be assured of our faith by its fruits and by our reverent behavior may win our neighbors to Christ." We don't have to think only of winning the neighbor to Christ to be persuaded that only in relationship to my neighbor can I attain this needed assurance of salvation. In his *Studies in Dogmatics,* Professor Berkouwer never tires of reminding us of this relationship.

That is to say, others must be able to say that I've delivered them out of the deceit, hypocrisy, shedding of blood, crime, and bribery mentioned in this Psalm. How good it would be—and that's the catechism's point—if I not only delivered someone *out of* all this but *from* all this, not only from wicked people but from wickedness itself because he sees me in terms of something else.

In what rewarding manner the phrase "But as for me" then comes into view, precisely for the wicked.

Others must be able to say that I have associated with them redemptively. To put it more strongly, Christ must be able to say that, as I have done it to the least of my brethren, I have done it to him (Matt. 25:40). Recalling how Jesus said that at the day of judgment this promise will be heard by the righteous with a question mark (i.e., they'll hear it with surprise), someone may suggest that the confidence of our Psalm sounds dreary and pharisaical compared with that question mark. That misses the point again, for the central word in our Psalm is not only "altar" but (if that's really different) "wondrous deeds" (vs. 7). We must not pit the New Testament against the Old Testament, the astonishment of the one against the astonishment of the other. It doesn't work.

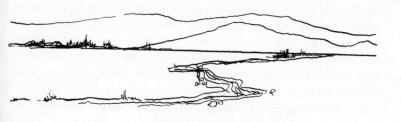

THE GREAT AND THE SMALL HEART

"Wait for the Lord;
be strong, and let your heart take courage;
yea, wait for the Lord!"

—Psalm 27:14

Expectation is a great word. It can also be an uncertain word. For example: "It might freeze and it might thaw" or "We'll have to wait and see." That's the way we meet it every day when we read the newspaper or turn on the radio. We'll have to wait and see—about the Common Market, about the disarmaments talks, or about the attitude of Brezhnev, or about the future of K.L.M., or about the expected freeze. Expectation is only a great and certain word when it's drawn from the Bible. Otherwise for our Psalm to speak of to "be strong" and to "take courage" would be out of the question. Expecting has nothing to do here with "wait and see," but it has everything to do with "counting on it."

It was demonstrated at Bethlehem

How can we have an intrepid heart? How can we have it in a time when there's so much loneliness that even families seem to provide little protection against it? Have there ever been so many roads torn up in a time when we might have expected the opposite? Have we ever been so socially concerned—and so a-socially? In a time when so much violence threatens, how can we have an intrepid heart?

For one thing, we can recognize that our Psalm is familiar with

the attitudes and situations just described. The Preacher is right
—there is not much new under the sun. Indeed, there is *nothing*
new under the sun (Eccles. 1:9). Notice how loneliness leers at
us in verse 10, where the poet reckons with being forsaken as by
his father and mother, being cut off from his past—a past that has
been torn up. We can guess that roads are torn up when he prays
in verse 11: "Teach me thy way, O LORD; and lead me on a level
path." There's mention of violence in the following verse as we
share his sigh: "Give me not up to the will of my adversaries."
All this gains our confidence. My loneliness, my anxieties, and
my fears are not mine alone but are known to all. I don't face
them alone. I'm part of a whole company, part of a past that can
talk about these things with me because it knows all about them.
That makes my own heart a little less fainthearted!

But my heart only takes courage by trusting in the Lord, for
that's what is meant by "wait for the LORD." Who is the Lord?
What is so special about Him that I should trust Him with all my
heart and being? The First Letter of John answers this. There we
read that God has a heart "greater than our hearts" (1 John
3:20). This is not said to frighten us. Seen in its context this is
precisely why we can be strengthened. It means neither more nor
less than that God's heart is big enough for us to enter in with
our hearts.

Where can this be demonstrated? Where has it been demonstrated once for all? If not in Bethlehem then I don't know anything any longer. If anywhere it's been shown how great is God's
heart and how it beats for us, then there! "Seek ye my face," we
read in our Psalm. Where better than in Bethlehem? Where can
we recognize God's face more intimately and clearly and confidently than in the face of the child of Bethlehem and in what he
let us see during his whole life on earth?

Henceforth, when someone dares us to show him God, we may
no longer reply that this is impossible. To be sure, I cannot let
God be seen. But He can do it Himself and He has shown Himself in truly poignant manner, in Jesus Christ. If someone asks us
to show him this God of ours, we will reply eagerly that it can

happen. And we'll never grow weary of pointing him to Jesus
Christ (John 1:18; 1 John 1:1).

The crown from the head

Actually, that impressive verse about God being "greater than
our hearts" says something more. It's the secret of our Psalm, although the poet doesn't make a point of this explicitly. It means
that God's heart is only greater than our heart if "our hearts condemn us." That means we must have a little heart, else we can't
get in. That must be why the three kings cast their crowns before
Him, and why this still happens when we sing in church "We
praise thee, thou holy lamb of God."

If we seek God's face seriously, as in this Psalm, it could
scarcely be otherwise. Whoever seeks this face seriously begins to
see what Peter saw when—for the first time in his life or at least
as never before—he saw with whom he had to do. What did Peter
see? We don't know exactly and we must not be curious. At any
rate, it affected him so much that "he went out and wept bitterly"
(Luke 22:62).

What is the worst?

If our life includes confession of sin, as in this Psalm, or if our
life is a confession of sin, it's also much more. Then we'll be able
to take it.

I'll be able to take it when "my father and my mother have forsaken me," when I feel cut off from my roots and there's no way
back, when all bridges have been burned. But that's not yet the
worst that can happen to me. Just so long as I'm not forsaken by
God (for then life would be unbearable)! Just so long as there's
One who says, "I am the way, and the truth, and the life" (John
14:6)! Just so long as there's no threat or wrath for me from that
direction! That would be the worst.

In other words, just so long as everything—all the forsakenness, all the brokenness, all the threats that can torment a man

(the poet doesn't deny these for he knows all about them)—can land *in God's heart* instead of falling outside the word of another Psalm which encloses sorrow like a lariat: "Thou dost beset me behind and before" (Ps. 139:5).

Of course, this is bound up with whether we really are aware that this God-forsakenness, this inability to reach Jesus any more, this recognition of heaven as hostile—that this is the worst a man has to shun in life or in death. In other words, we have to shun *sin* as the worst thing there is, thus expressing agreement with our confession of faith (Sunday 2 of the Heidelberg Catechism) which sees sin as the epitome of our misery. Or take Lamentations. In a climate of such utter wretchedness that we wouldn't blame anyone for hardly thinking of something like sin, it's striking to hear suddenly, "How a man complains of his life! Everyone complains about his sin!" (3:39, Dutch version). If I don't reckon with the abandonment, the brokenness, and the enmity of sin, I won't be able to make it in the safety of my home (no matter how happy), or in my way (no matter how smooth), or in the cold war (no matter how peaceful). All this could merely take me farther away from God's great heart. On the other hand, if I reckon with the fullness of God, with His ways and with His reconciliation, then every misery will but draw me nearer to God's heart (Sunday 1 of the Heidelberg Catechism).

Here and hereafter

Speaking of a strong and intrepid heart, one of the strongest examples of that heart is an expression in the Psalm we have not yet examined and which we must not pass by, if only because it has become one of the most cherished expressions of the church: "I believe that I shall see the goodness of the LORD in the land of the living!" The expression is striking because it puts the glorious promise of the Psalm on *this* side, and not in the hereafter. No Jew would do the latter because he felt such a strong tie to the here and now. If a Jew would not jump over the present and all the glorious things God has bound to it, a Christian must not do it either. There are differences enough between the one and the other, between the Old Testament and the New—but these differences must never be understood as though the one had a concern for the present while the other was only concerned with the hereafter. Both Old and New Testament know both sides. As though God were only the God of "the other side"! As though Bethlehem did not happen precisely on our side and in the midst of our life! As though the "tent" spoken of in verse 5 is any other than the manger spoken of in Luke 2:7! Isn't what happened at Christmas what occurs in our Psalm—a festival of the forgiveness of sins and all the warmth, safety, and trust that are part of it? Where else could forgiveness occur if not on "this" side? Isn't this "the goodness of the LORD" par excellence? Isn't this where God's heart is most fully revealed? In a life that can turn against me in ever so many ways (vss. 10-12), what avails is a God who is for me (Rom. 8:31).

Of course we can experience the Lord's goodness in this life. I must not think it could be otherwise! Were this not so we would be as poor as those who think of eternal life only as something that begins after death, whereas it begins whenever they wish . . .

Then, and only then, may I also say more and believe more— namely, that God's "steadfast love is better than life," better than this life (Ps. 63:3). This life is too small for it, when "the former things have passed away" (Rev. 21:4). At times we get the impression that we've only reached the letter *a* in the whole alphabet of God's wonders.

But then too, no matter how much progress I may have made, my heart will always be smaller than His—else I would not have life anymore—not now and not ever.

THE SILENT GOD

"To thee, O Lord, I call;
my rock, be not deaf to me . . ."

—Psalm 28:1

That God can be silent—*can* be, for surely that's not all He is —is a well-known problem. And not only in this Psalm. In Psalm 39:12, we hear the poet say: "hold not thy peace at my tears!" and in Psalm 83:1: "O God, do not keep silence; do not hold thy peace or be still, O God!" This holds some comfort—however meager—for us who sometimes think the silent God is a modern discovery, a fate that only now hangs somberly over the world. A little historical perspective, especially a little church-historical perspective from the Bible, can help us. This sense of loneliness is certainly a problem but not a particularly modern problem. Who do we think we are!

No one answered

Not a modern problem—but certainly a problem! Where else have we heard about a god who was silent? I write a small "g" intentionally, and that's already a clue. It's the familiar story of Elijah on Mount Carmel, a story we first heard as children. On that occasion, we know how Elijah made fun of his rivals, the servants of Baal, when they tried in vain to arouse their god from slumber. Their entreaties simply re-echoed: "O Baal, answer us!" But there was no voice and no one answered (1 Kings 18:26).

The question that brings us into temptation is this—might God
be one of the false gods? Or, and no less frightening—might we
belong to the ungodly? That's the problem with which this Psalm
and our daily life vex us, even if the poet had other ungodly men
in mind than ourselves.

Various answers

Why would the Lord God do this? Why would He keep silence? Various answers are possible. An element of punishment
may be hidden in the silence of God. God is angry and will not
make contact. Psalm 39:8 makes us think of this because the
poet speaks of his own transgressions along with the silence of
God. There may well be a relationship between silence and punishment. The silence of God may also contain an element of testing. I don't think that the way Job met this silence of God allows
us to see a direct relation with punishment. On the contrary, those
who did this were themselves punished (Job 42:7-9)!

Incomprehensible grace

When we think of punishment or testing, of a silence of God
"because" or of a silence of God "so that," we think of something
that happens occasionally. God doesn't always punish, nor does
He test Job forever. After forty-one chapters of raw misery comes
a happy ending. But we can also speak of a silence of God that
surrounds Him eternally—a mystery that accompanies Him eternally and which doesn't completely vanish in redemption, the
mystery par excellence. We're speaking of God's incomprehensibility. This must be distinguished from unknowability. God is certainly knowable, most unhappily in His general revelation and
most happily in His special revelation. This doesn't affect His incomprehensibility, though perhaps we should make this a distinction instead of a separation. There is a silence of God which is
another name for His incomprehensibility. We'll have to learn to
live with that. Indeed, we'll have to live with that forever.

However much the Son may have revealed to us about the depths of the Father—His redemption (Matt. 11:27)—and however much we too, thanks to the former, have learned of the latter (John 1:18), Paul can still write Timothy about God as One "who alone has immortality and dwells in unapproachable light, whom no man has ever seen or can see." That didn't give him any less reason to praise and glorify this God. On the contrary! He adds, "To him be honor and eternal dominion! Amen" (1 Tim. 6:16). This silence about God corresponds to silence about the deepest springs of our own existence—ultimately incomprehensible because they are pure grace—as well as about the deepest springs of God's existence. It's of the greatest importance that we cannot wholly fathom either of these—and of course there's a link between them. Ultimately our life is suspended on a mystery. Not one commentator would take 1 Corinthians 13:12 (". . . then I shall understand fully, even as I have been fully understood") except as a *human* knowledge of God that has nothing to do with pride but has everything to do with gratitude.

A wretched interpretation

The fact that we can properly associate the silence of God with His incomprehensibility must not tempt us to start attributing all sorts of incomprehensible things to God. The Psalmist, who certainly was aware of God's incomprehensibility, doesn't try to blame God for all sorts of incomprehensible things with which he's faced—such as the fact that his life is almost choked by the wicked, people who don't mean it when their lips say friendly things, not to mention the "scandalous conduct" of which he also speaks. He doesn't fret about this. He's not a "monist" as we would say today (= thinking that everything, including sorrow and all the most bitter experiences, reduce to one common denominator of God). That's why he can ask God defiantly why He doesn't step in.

Meantime, we know from the Old Testament message that not only is God active in the drama on earth, but that there are two

in the drama—God and the *devil*! Job 1:6 and 2:1 can tell us
more about that. We have a good example of the devil's presence
in the storm at sea (Mark 4:35-41). It's a good example because
that story begins with something familiar to us from the Psalm—
that God is silent. Jesus sleeps, and that's certainly a particular
form of silence! We discover too that the disciples didn't understand, and the story ends with a rebuke to the storm as though it
concealed something or "someone," making us think of the devil.
Not that the latter is responsible for the silent God. God Himself is
responsible for that—or we. But the devil is responsible for the
wretched interpretation with which he provides us, one we often
accept all too eagerly!

The right address

That story of the storm at sea as a variation of our poet's
theme, as a familiar story of the silent God, can teach us something else—not about the devil but about ourselves. It's not only
the devil who is rebuked in this story. So are disciples—and not
just a little! We hear Jesus say, "Why . . . Have you no faith?"
(Mark 4:40).

What should they have done had they rightly used their faith?
They must have had faith, else Jesus would not have been so angry. For one thing, they should not have taken his silence as a
deafness, for that's not the same thing at all. We should take that
into account in the translation of Psalm 28:1, for "He who planted
the ear, does he not hear?" (Ps. 94:9). Surely they should not
have thought that a Lord who sleeps is any less a Lord. It may be
that the poet of our Psalm may think of this momentarily—as
does the poet of Psalm 83:1, for whom the silence of God is the
same as His inactivity—although our poet contradicts this by con-
tinuing to address as "a rock" the God he accuses of being silent!
He does what Job often did—resists the God to whom he clings,
puts question marks after a God whom he decorates with exclamation points! In the last analysis, such contending is the same as
loving. All through the Psalm we meet such swaying back and

forth in the faith of a believer—asking and thanking, thanking and asking. (Compare verses 1-5, 6-8, and 9.) Even in its doubt the worship of the church knows how to glorify God because it knows the right address for this doubt.

In this sense, God is honored even in our doubt, and even disciples honor Him, no matter how much they are rebuked. When help came, it came to them as friends.

Maturity

Perhaps they could have done something else with their faith besides trusting that a Jesus who sleeps is no less Jesus, and that a God who is silent is no less God. Luke 9:41 gives us a clue. There Jesus rebukes disciples for lack of faith because they could not heal one who was sick. Jesus is furious with them because He had given them faith enough for it! Perhaps God's silence amid all sorts of miseries means that we shouldn't be running head over heels to Him with our lack of faith, but instead, with our sufficient faith, should tackle the miseries, exorcise storms, and heal the sick. This may smack of the fanaticism of faith healers, but no harm is done if occasionally these come into the church's view.

When all is said and done, the Lord God has every reason to be silent occasionally. He certainly has done His part! Surely, we can and must see it this way since the Word has become flesh (John 1:14) and since God has said all He has to say in the fullest sense of this word (Heb. 1:1). He has literally exhausted Himself by telling us everything He had to say in Jesus Christ, the dearest and strongest and best He had. There is a silence of God that makes a Christian mature and puts him on his feet and gives him voice.

Of course we must express this maturity. Even after God has said all He has to say in Jesus Christ, when He has every reason to be silent, even then we're not above worrying like the poet who, after his spirited confession in verse 7, again implores to be "carried" (vs. 9). It might be well for us to think here not of a lamb being carried by a shepherd but of a son being carried by his father (Deut. 1:31). The father delegates a lot to the son, but the son doesn't worry about not relying on the father anymore. If indeed the one "carried" in our Psalm is a king (verse 8 speaks of an "anointed"), a king who realizes his dependence, and if this king can point us to another in Gethsemane (Matt. 26:37), then *we* have no cause to be offended. What does Jesus' sojourn on earth mean if it doesn't provoke us to Christian maturity, to an undergirding of that maturity through the outpouring of the Holy Spirit?

There is a dark side to the silence of God. If He should go through with it, it would mean death for me. The poet is right. Then I would become "like those who go down to the Pit." But there's also a glorious side to it full of promise—a "do it yourself!" Especially after Jesus said "It is finished" there is an especially exciting explanation for the silence of God—our own coming of age. In that sense, we can speak not only of the problem but also and especially of the *gospel* of the silent God.

"Upon the housetops"

Finally, how little God intends His silence to be fatal is evident in the poet's behavior and in ours when it really matters. Luther is right when he says of this Psalm: "God Himself isn't so inclined, though in the hearts of believers it may seem to be so." We have a striking example of this in Gethsemane. Who was asleep when it really mattered as never before? Who was silent then—He or I?

We were asleep (Matt. 26:40). This will teach us to quote Psalm 28:1 sparingly, to understand the hidden meaning (the good news) of God's silence, and to shout it "upon the housetops" (Matt. 10:27).

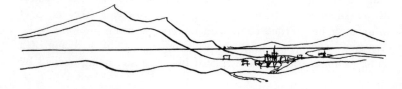

THE VOICE AND THE THUNDER

"The voice of the Lord is upon the waters; the God of glory thunders . . ."

—Psalm 29:3

Nowadays we have difficulty with this text—indeed, with the whole Psalm. We like to secularize nature, things, history—to demythologize, despiritualize, materialize everything. For most of us thunder has become just plain, ordinary thunder, and no longer the voice of the Lord, as in this Psalm. The same holds true for those fiery arrows shot by Yahweh (Pss. 18:14; 77:17). We prefer to speak simply of lightning.

No dilemma

There's a lot to say for this. Thunder really is also ordinary thunder. If we try too quickly and eagerly to make it the voice of the Lord we might forget this and begin to deify the elements.

Still, the opposite error is no less error. Just as the voice of the Lord does not keep thunder from being thunder, so thunder must not exclude the fact that what ultimately matters is the voice of the Lord. When it comes to bread, the baker and the Lord must not become rivals. If we visit a zoo, we may say that a giraffe is a droll animal, but we may also say that the Lord God has made him droll. We must not create a dilemma where none exists. Who or what actually helped us to victory in 1945? Was it the fact that the allies had more oil than the Germans, or was it the Lord God? In our services of thanksgiving that was no problem.

Against mythology

There's more to be said. The Psalm we want to demythologize is itself an enormous protest against mythology!

N. H. Ridderbos, as many others, points out that the Psalm may be adapted from a hymn to the West-Semitic god of thunder, Baal-Hadad, who has become better known to us through excavations at Ugarit. But, he adds, the change of name, Yahweh instead of Baal-Hadad, points to an enormous difference in meaning. In the world surrounding Israel deification of nature and of the elements was the order of the day. Baal-Hadad was a deified power of nature. But under the power of Yahweh, nature and the elements are desacralized in Israel. That makes a great difference!

Accordingly, in our Psalm nature doesn't war against man or against itself. God carries on His battle in and over "nature." Böhl says: "The mighty waters which are drowned out and brought to silence by the divine voice in the thunder are symbol of the powers of chaos and disorder that were vanquished by God in the beginning of the creation." The threatening power of water is well known to us in our ordinary life and in that of other peoples, cultures, and religions. Lamparter too, referring to our Psalm, points out how often in the Old Testament water symbolizes the world of nations that rebel against God. He points to Psalm 93. But also in the cedars of Lebanon (which, according to our Psalm, are terror-stricken) he sees all sorts of exalted pride and boasting on earth that need to be shattered—pointing us to Isaiah 2:12-13, where the cedars of Lebanon are actually named in such arrogant connection. Ridderbos too notes that what is struck by lightning in our Psalm are not the arable land or the cities of Israel but the sea, the mountain heights, the wilderness and the forests, and these in turn represent antagonistic and mysterious powers. At any rate, he concludes, they often meant this to Israel.

Dumbfounded

In this connection Ridderbos even suggests the possibility that the so-called "heavenly beings" of verse 1 should be translated differently because they refer not to angels but to gods, to the vanquished gods of the heathen. He reads Psalm 138:1 in the same way.

At first sight we would not have thought of that. At first sight we would think of angels summoned to praise. Aren't they always near when God appears in His glory? When Job is made aware of God's might, we hear God say that the morning stars sang together and that all the sons of God shouted for joy (38:7). Of what or of whom do we think when we pray, "Thy will be done, On earth *as it is in heaven*," if not angels?

A transition from this more familiar view to that of Ridderbos may be possible through the well-known verse from the *Te Deum*: "To thee all angels cry aloud; the heavens, and all the powers. To thee cherubim and seraphim continually do cry." That is to say, along with seraphim and angels, the "domestic" ministering spirits of God, all powers and thrones of the world are summoned to place themselves under God's dominion. They are dumbfounded by His word of power.

Meaningless

How do we know this? I've said it already—through His word. We don't know this from thunder itself. We must not equate thunder with the voice of the Lord or we'll end up with the heathen. All the critics we've mentioned are right in rejecting this equation and identification. Thunder itself has no voice. It makes a lot of noise but doesn't say anything. It's true that thunder has had a lot to say among us. Once we even made a god out of it, but nowadays Donar is silent and only the God of Israel still speaks. That's the difference between the gods and the God of Israel: "They have mouths, but they speak not" (Ps. 135:16). But He speaks —how He speaks! We know it from this word. That's where the poet got it. From where? From his palace, he says. Today we would say in the church. That's where God is worshiped for what He does with *His* thunder, not wielding it at random but in such a way that the tremor on earth begins to sing in lower key instead of merely shouting. Hengstenberg has put this very well: "The greatness of God in the thunderstorm is portrayed for us only so that in this way a shield is prepared for the church against everything that arouses anxiety and fear." No wonder that in his commentary Luther not only agrees with the Psalmist's preference for speaking of the voice of the Lord instead of the voice of the thunder but that he goes on to suggest that the former should be understood as the preaching of the gospel, the most convulsive power that earth has ever known or experienced. Indeed. How will the Son of man come? As lightning (Matt. 24:27)!

Glorified

Speaking of the gospel, we have related but distinguished thunder and the voice of the Lord. We need both to relate and to distinguish them if we're to understand the following story.

After his entry into Jerusalem Jesus speaks once more, now with the emphasis on his death. He is deeply moved and prays for the Father's approval of his redemptive work. We read the reply: "Then a voice came from heaven, 'I have glorified it, and I will glorify it again.' " That isn't all. The evangelist adds: "The crowd standing by heard it and said that it had thundered" (John 12:28-29).

Perhaps now the relation as well as the distinction between thunder and the voice of the Lord is no longer such a problem for us.

PREDESTINATION

*"For his anger is but for a moment,
and his favor is for a lifetime"*

—Psalm 30:5

N. H. Ridderbos translates our text: "For a sudden plague comes by his anger, but life by his good pleasure." That doesn't change the meaning so far as it concerns the delightful difference between the first and second parts of our text, the difference between God's anger and His favor. Nor does this text stand alone. What immediately follows says the same: "Weeping may tarry for the night, but joy comes with the morning." In other words, God changed His mind about it in a single night and once again the new day lies radiantly open (cf. Isa. 17:14). In Isaiah 54:8 we meet something as similar to our text as two peas in a pod: "In overflowing wrath for a moment I hid my face from you, but with everlasting love I will have compassion on you." That God's anger is but for a little while plays a large role in Zechariah 1:15. There we read that the hostile nations extended God's wrath unnecessarily and irresponsibly. Our text is evidently part and parcel with the whole of the biblical message.

What a difference!

What a difference! The difference doesn't lie in the fact that God's anger only lasts five minutes while His grace lasts a lifetime. No. We've seen that the first also accompanies us all our life! However, *in comparison with* the other, this relationship is no relationship at all or, at most, only as a moment to eternity (cf. 2 Cor. 4:17). That makes the difference greater, not less. What a difference! It's the difference between what God likes to do and what He doesn't like to do, between what He chooses and what He rejects. Again it was Luther who made an excellent comment on this text: "God the Father hates sin and death and cannot bear them, for He did not create death and He does not delight in the destruction of the ungodly . . . God is reluctant about this anger, He takes . . . pleasure in life."

The difference lies in the fact that God's anger comes on our account while His grace is on His account. We could say that His anger is wrung from Him while His grace is poured out royally to us. One must not object that, were something wrung from Him, this would reduce His doing and permitting to a mere reaction to our own doing and permitting, and thus would be inconsistent with His sovereignty. It's possible to argue that God doesn't react, but it's also possible to argue that He does react and that no one can react as well as He. In that case, it's not at the expense of His sovereignty for this penetrates it through and through!

As "irrational" as He is in His grace, so "rational" is He in His anger. The first has no occasion; the second has. Look at our text. God's grace is experienced as a miracle, but His anger as a perfectly understandable affair. After all, the poet asked for it! How is clear enough. "I said in my prosperity, 'I shall never be moved.'" That is to say, his prosperity had gone to his head, whereas God's "favor" was the reason his "strong mountain" had been established. That's how he had lost sight of his God ("thou didst hide thy face, I was dismayed"). But notice. He is pronounced healed again!

Period, comma

I've written these last lines quite intentionally, especially those concerning the "rational" character of God's anger. Just as a given text can take us into politics one moment and into the church the next moment, so this text takes us into dogmatic theology. In our text something essential is said about God's anger—it's this: God's anger is not like His grace. We've often tried and we still try to defend the contrary by a particular, symmetrical attempt to speak of a "double" predestination. Happily this attempt is rejected with quite as much or more emphasis. Happily this isn't only true nowadays (for example, in his book on election Professor Berkouwer demonstrates that the symmetry between salvation and judgment is already broken by the fact that God sent His Son into the world not to condemn but to save). It was also true formerly (for example, while retaining the concept of "double" predestination, Bavinck emphasized that the "pre" words in the Bible are used exclusively with reference to predestination to glory). Indeed, it is already true much earlier (for example, though in our opinion the Canons of Dort are open to a great deal of misunderstanding, we should notice that they specifically deny "that *in the same manner* in which the election is the fountain and cause of faith and good works, reprobation is the cause of unbelief and impiety").

We might wonder whether the "one" predestination doesn't so excel and trump the "other" that it negates the latter altogether. If we trace the history of the Jewish people in the Bible we get a strong impression of the *incidental* character of God's judgment and of those damning words used about it there. There's always a comma after the judgment, never a period. More precisely, the period always turns out to be a comma after all. This applies not only to the Jewish people *in* the Bible. Romans 9—11 tells us that this must determine our view of the Jewish people *today*.

No wonder that Barth, in whose theology God's grace is so triumphant that resisting it to eternity will not avail us, uses our text frequently.

All the more serious

We must not counter this by saying that the Bible is also acquainted with the "other" sound. For example, Proverbs 16:4 says: "The Lord has made everything for its purpose, even the wicked for the day of trouble." We cannot infer more from this text than that the wicked and the day of trouble belong together, as do the righteous and the day of salvation. Gispen, referring to 2 Corinthians 5:11, adds that this proverb expressly wants to arouse the wicked to repentance through fear of the coming judgment! Yet we cannot deny that Psalm 30:6, for all its refreshing content and breathtaking contrast, *can be nullified*—not by a double predestination in the symmetrical sense of the word, but by a "sure" opposition of grace. We had to avoid this idea over against the Remonstrants (and rightly so), and we have to bring it out of the arsenal again against Barth (and rightly so). However, the decisive character of faith needs to be wielded over against the former in a different manner than over against the latter. In recent theology the relation is not between acquittal and guilt but between guilt and acquittal. That's why the "hardening" texts play a greater role than ever, not so much in terms of judgmental initiative on God's part as in terms of a guilty initiative on man's part and, for that reason, a judgmental reaction on God's part. This, it seems to me, is wholly within the spirit of our text. The rejection in our text can never be enclosed *in it* as provocation to do so. Quite the contrary. So much the worse if this happens nonetheless.

A terrible sin

We had better let go of the idea of double predestination. While in His reaction God doesn't allow the initiative out of His hand, the word "predestination" doesn't fit here very well. We do better to use the biblical word "hardening." That sounds more incidental and less primary. It speaks of something wrung from God. If we want to give it more content, let's not speak of a predestination *of God* to evil but *of our own*. God Himself has never intended on evil in any way, but we have. Listen: "These have chosen their own ways, and their soul delights in their abominations; I also will choose afflictions for them" (Isa. 66:3-4). The judgment of God doesn't correspond to His favor but only to our guilt.

That's what the text says. We're not free to nullify it. It remains a terrible sin, the sin against the Holy Spirit.

ROOM

"Into thy hand I commit my spirit ..."

—Psalm 31:5

Evidently the poet is having a hard time. That's why the Psalm has the title "Prayer in Distress" in the new translation of the Netherlands Bible Society. Exactly what the distress was we do not know. Some have thought of the enmity between Saul and David, but one could think as easily of all sorts of enmity, and sickness has also been suggested. I don't think the last can be refuted simply by the fact that the poet's grief is displayed publicly ("those who see me in the street flee from me"!), for a great deal of sickness can be seen publicly. Luther tells us that in times of illness he found a great deal of help in this Psalm, especially in verse 15 ("My times are in thy hand"). On the other hand, expressions like "my eye is wasted from grief, my soul and my body also" need not refer to illness. We recognize these symptoms, these psychosomatic catalogues of misery, from the war years. We'll have to leave it at that. Whatever it was, the poet feels like "a broken vessel." We could say about his life—what a pity! How useless! The worst of it in fact, is that we *do* talk like this!

The safe

Much more important than what *we* say is what *he* says. He says: "Into thy hand I commit my spirit."

The word "hand" recurs in our Psalm. We could say there are
many hands—the hands of enemies, vulture hands that scratch
and claw, a frightening picture. Amid all these hands he discovers
others which are the very picture of trust—father hands, nuptial
hands, hands that comfort. He commits his spirit to these hands.
That is to say, he places his spirit in these hands as we would
place our capital, everything we have, in a bank safe and, having
done so, return to the street with a sigh of relief.

A lot can still happen to us—but no one will be able to touch
that. And what is this "spirit"? I've said it already. It's my life's
capital, the principal, the foundation, the soul, the spunk, the faith
—it's all one and the same. It's that with which I stand or fall.

Obviously, this depositing has nothing to do with resignation.
It's much too active for that. I have to go to the bank myself!
Moreover, it accomplishes too much for that. Our text is followed
immediately by: "Thou dost redeem me, O Lord, faithful God."
We can even read it: "Thou *hast* redeemed me, O Lord, faithful
God." That doesn't mean recalling something from the past—a
believer's experience—although of course it will include that. It
means we can already transport ourselves out of present distress
into the coming redemption as if it were already behind us.

We know such anticipation plays a role not only here but all
through the Bible. I think especially of what we read at the end of
the Bible, where there's talk of a time when there will be no more
death, "neither . . . mourning nor crying nor pain," following
which we read that these glorious things *have* already happened
(Rev. 21:4-6)!

Dying before one's time

A text like this should not make us think only of death and of
resurrection and of our entrance into the new earth—or that in
all sorts of death today we should anticipate already all sorts of
resurrection and already see all sorts of places on this new earth.
How pitiful if we only began to commit our spirit into God's
hands at the hour of death in order to count on a redemption afterward! The Psalmist doesn't do this. We must not use a text

like "My times are in thy hand" (vs. 15) in this way either. To be sure, it's also a word we often find on tombstones, even as our text is often used in time of death, but we must not limit it to such circumstances. Again, how pitiful that would be! Commenting on this text, Luther said he once was inclined to think of the hour of death but that he had turned away from this interpretation. There are other hours than the hour of our death. Suppose *these* were not in God's hand! Although Luther doesn't refer to it, he is surely thinking of Romans 8:38-39 ("For I am sure that neither death, nor life . . . will be able to separate us from the love of God"). We must not be so "pious" as to think only of dying. Bonhoeffer told us we must not try to be a step behind God or a step ahead of Him. We can learn, and unlearn, a great deal from Israel on this point! Israel can break us of thinking too soon about dying and also of going to death too soon. Ecclesiastes 7:17 reminds us that a man can even die "before his time." Might one not be bound to the other—thinking too much about death and going to death too soon? It's interesting to note that Ecclesiastes speaks of this not in connection with piety but in connection with wickedness.

Set in a large room

All this is not to deny that we may also utter this word when distress is greatest, in the hour of death. We should not be ashamed to grasp for it then. The greatest Israelite we known did this when He said, "Father, into thy hands I commit my spirit" (Luke 23:46). That was when this Psalm found a special fulfillment, as terrible as it was glorious.

How He was tormented—and not only by His enemies! How He became a reproach to His "neighbors"! Think of Peter who denied Him, and of Judas who betrayed Him. Think how He became "an object of dread" (vs. 11) to His "acquaintances," and how those who saw Him fled from Him (Mark 14:50)! But how glorious! How glorious was His trust when within a distress we can only begin to imagine but which for Him was bitter reality— that of being forsaken by God—He did not breathe His last breath wildly but committed it to His *Father*. And how glorious was the outcome when His feet were set "in a large room" (vs. 8, K.J.V.) as He arose and ascended to heaven!

What a breakthrough

There is something utterly realistic and prophetic about this Psalm. Pleading and thanksgiving, fear and trust, both continue in this life of ours. According to N. H. Ridderbos, our Psalm is a striking example of a dialectic that governs our life (cf. verses 1-8 and 9-24). Twice we make the transition from one to the other. How a believer can sway back and forth!

This characteristic note of our Psalm, as Ridderbos points out, can also help us with the question of how it's possible for one man to experience this at every moment. Aside from the fact that it is possible, we sense in this Psalm, as in all the Psalms, the experience of the church of every age, swaying back and forth between pain and healing, between pleading and thanksgiving, between fear and trust, between doubt and faith. In other words these Psalms express more than the life experience of *one* believer; they express a liturgy of redemption by the church of all ages. One could compare the abrupt way in which the proclamation of grace each Sunday tumbles over the confession of sin. This need not characterize one's own experience at the moment so long as it characterizes the experience of the faithful of all ages.

However, the faithful of all ages have instinctively known that the last (belief and trust, healing and thanksgiving) will here too be the first. One day we'll all be set in a broad place, in the fullest transparency. Already we hear about a "sea of glass" (Rev. 15:2). We might expect transparency from a sea, but we also hear about "streets of glass" (Rev. 21:21). This we had not expected. In contrast to our present life where everything is regularly locked up and shut tight and which can be oppressive until death, the gates of that life will always stand open (Rev. 21:25). What a breakthrough! It will be like a constant birth, one blessed event!

LIBERATION

". . . thou dost encompass me with deliverance."

—Psalm 32:7

Liberation is a wonderful word—in fact, a wonderful celebration which we in Holland observe every year. The Psalmist is also acquainted with the concept of liberation, albeit in a very particular context. The context makes clear what kind of liberation is meant. It's precisely the clarity of this context which liberation-in-general prefers to forget, leaving it troubled and ambiguous. That even makes our own wonderful celebration every year a bit tragic. The liberation we celebrate each year since 1945 is never as complete as that which the poet celebrates. That, as the context tells us, is liberation from sin. That's quite a context for it's a long road.

The long road

The context tells us that for a long time the poet has been silent about what really matters if liberation is to be complete. We learn that then his situation had become unbearable, that he had become frantic about it, that something had been strangling his life, that he had broken out in a sweat. The great relief and true liberation only came with the confession of his sin. We get the impression that it didn't just happen. It must have been a long road—all the way from verse 3 to verse 7, for there's a tremendous difference between the former silence and the later jubilation. Something had really happened!

We know what actually did happen better than did the poet. We know what this long road from verse 3 to verse 7 entailed. It is the way of Golgotha. We know precisely what happened. It took a cross (and what a cross!), and it took a resurrection (and what a resurrection!). We know precisely what drops of sweat and what hammer blows made it possible to come out of greatest dread into great jubilation. That's how it became possible.

It can still happen

And now, what of our "liberation"? It's also a wonderful word but the context is different. Ever since 1945 it seems as though we've not wholly come out of dread or wholly into liberation. We've been stuck somewhere in the middle in a relative celebration in a cold war. That may be because the link between our liberation and that of the poet is only relative—liberation from the Germans over against liberation from our sins. That's not the same thing!

Has the West come sufficiently to liberation from sin? We don't get that impression, and not only in Germany. We rather get the impression that the West would like nothing better than to deliver the East from *its* sins. Newspaper and radio do not give the impression that we also need to be delivered from a great deal. We can find this needed sense of sin in the churches, but they usually fall back on such a general confession of sin that at most we hear "alas" but seldom "woe." And isn't the difference between West and East that the West still knows something about sin and has a consciousness of sin, even a Christian consciousness? It makes little sense to reproach the West for the West itself is nothing. The West is people, and they are something. At any rate, according to the poet, they are something if they understand liberation as liberation from sin. We have a fairly good idea of what Moscow and Peking mean by freedom, and for that reason what we do *not* mean by it. But we have only a poor idea of what Paul means by it—the freedom of the Holy Spirit that consists in "love, joy, peace, patience, kindness, goodness, faithfulness, gentleness, self-control" (Gal. 5:22-23). Anyone who lets himself be liberated by God receives all this in exchange.

We must not suppose that we're free to determine our own freedom or that this can just go on. God still lets Himself be found. The poet suggests this will not always be the case. Let me put it this way: now it's still possible with good grace but later it will happen willy-nilly, with "bit and bridle" (vs. 9)—or not at all. What happened to Esau would then happen to us. "For you know that afterward, when he desired to inherit the blessing, he was rejected, for he found no chance to repent, though he sought it with tears" (Heb. 12:17). That's a terrible word, especially if we read deliverance for repentance. Evidently he had no idea of sin and therefore no idea of deliverance from sin.

The hut and the rock

There are, of course, all sorts of liberation, and many are worth a great deal. But there is only one true liberation. That's why the poet is so jubilant and why we manage it so poorly.

Does this jubilation mean there won't be any more trouble? No, the word "trouble" appears right next to the word "deliverance" in our text. Troubles there are plenty, but we're protected from them—i.e. we're not lost in them and don't suffocate in them. When distress overtakes a man, when life has him by the throat, when the walls press in upon him, there's always still an open roof over his head—there's always still an ascension possible. That's what the road to Golgotha has taught us. That's where the road runs from verse 3 to verse 7. There is indeed trouble for the believer, else our text would not have to say: "Thou art a hiding place for me." But the hiding place is greater than the troubles, so much greater that we can speak of liberation and even of jubilation. We have the same in Psalm 27, where we hear not only about a hut which symbolizes a hiding place (as well as humility and confession of sin) but also about a rock which symbolizes courage (as well as openness and confidence). Perhaps we may conclude that the hut is identical with the rock. Only he who knows one knows the other. One who seeks God in his troubles, and especially for his worst trouble, sin, experiences joyous deliverance. We bow to get into a hut; we stand on a rock. When Mary had passed the night in the shelter of the Most High and in the shadow of the Almighty (Ps. 91:1), her song of praise and the angel choir come into view. Jubilation breaks forth after she has been delivered from her distress, "How can this be . . . ?" (Luke 1:34) with the words: "Behold I am the handmaid of the Lord; let it be to me according to your word" (Luke 1:38)! All generations shall call her blessed (Luke 1:48)!

What liberation from what trouble is the deliverance from all our sins, is encounter with Jesus!

So no more army?

What liberation from what trouble is the encounter with Him who shall save His people from their sins (Matt. 1:21)!

Does this mean no other liberation is important? Does it mean no more need for an army? In the Old Testament it doesn't have to be an either/or, just so long as we keep the distinction in mind. The soldier was neither luxury nor shame in Israel. In the last analysis, however, it's not armies that keep us from anxieties but "songs of deliverance." The Lord will be to us "a wall of fire round about," says Zechariah (2:5), even though he knows of other walls. The prophet wasn't averse to "power and might" for he says what he says in a city built with "trowel and sword." Yet *within* it he says: "Not by might, nor by power, but by my Spirit, says the Lord of hosts" (Zech. 4:6). If we let our liberation, however important, take the place of the ultimate liberation and fail to see it dependent on that—then we no longer deserve the name of a Christian West and we really don't know what liberation means.

Only one who understands liberation as deliverance from the greatest distress in life and in death, and who cannot keep silent about that, only such a person will never be brought to his knees by smaller distress.

We are the songs

Finally, who sings the jubilant songs of deliverance? We could say, God does, but we must not stop there because God doesn't stop there. What God does He does through people, even to the appearing of His beloved Son on earth. So He sings through us.

We have a good example of these things at Pentecost. How does the fire burn there? God makes it burn, but it burns on my head in such manner that everyone can see it. It's the same with those songs in which the fire also breaks out (the text really says, "screaming songs"). God encircles us with them, but we sing the songs and, we add, we *are* the songs. Unless we are to stay caught in sheer and therefore damned aesthetics in church, we must go on to say that we encircle *each other* like so many walls. That's how freely we can associate with each other. In the last analysis, that's what life is all about. In every anxiety we are to be each other's liberation, hiding place, and protection. No one delegates so wonderfully and completely as God does. That is the church.

So Jericho falls

This should not only be called protection; it's also the true assault. Our concern isn't simply the church but also and especially the world. Isn't that the way Jericho, the last stronghold of the foe, was conquered? Only so will the holy land lie open to us with its abundance of milk and honey. In the new covenant, in the time of mission and evangelism, we should understand this in terms of *people* whom we overcome with jubilant songs of deliverance. There's music in that!

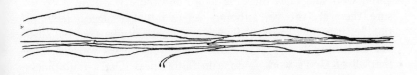

THE WORD OF THE LORD

*"By the word of the Lord the heavens were made,
and all of their host by the breath of his mouth."*

—Psalm 33:6

By the phrase "the word of the LORD" and all this may include as effect we don't usually think of creation first of all, as is the case in our Psalm. We usually think of that well-known word of the Lord that "became flesh" (John 1:14). There's good reason why this word has become so well known, but this must not let us forget the ordinary in the extraordinary, or let creation hide behind redemption. Even the word that "became flesh" is reminder of the word which "was in the beginning" (John 1:1-2). Creation is not because of redemption, though some have tried to tell us this lately. It's the other way around. Redemption is because of creation. Verses 6-9 in our Psalm are a clear reminder.

Creation and redemption

When we read these verses again, all of us think of the creation and the opening chapters of Genesis, especially Genesis 1:3: "And God said, 'Let there be light'; and there was light." To be sure, there are two verses before verses 6-9 that suggest redemption because they speak of justice and righteousness (out of injustice and unrighteousness). Yet in these very verses we also read that all of God's work is done in faithfulness. God's faithfulness doesn't make its appearance for the first time when redemption appears, but manifests itself already in creation. What else is redemption but God's stubborn faithfulness to creation? In such concepts as faithfulness, grace, covenant, we think of redemption in particular but of creation in general. That's true also of the word.

Word of faithfulness

The word of the Lord is the faithfulness of the Lord. Verse 9 brings this out in singular beauty: "For he spoke, and it came to be; he commanded, and it stood forth."

All this sounds very wonderful, even miraculous. For us the miraculous seems to lie especially in the suddenness. Someone says something—and the next moment it is so! However, I don't think the amazing part of this expression lies in the suddenness. Of course it *can* be sudden. I think of what happened when the centurion of Capernaum said of Jesus: "But say the word, and let my servant be healed" (Luke 7:1-10), and the servant was promptly healed. But it doesn't *have* to happen that way. No, the amazing part lies in the faithfulness. God sees to it that His word accomplishes His will. When it happens is secondary. *How* it happens is important but more important is *that* it happens. I'm not sure whether it's been tried but I am sure we must not use a text like this ("For he spoke, and it came to be; he commanded, and it stood forth") against evolution which has taught us that whatever exists on earth has been brought into being gradually. God takes the means so seriously that He doesn't like to omit them. It's part of the nature of creating that to a large extent creation is left to itself so that it may lead its own life.

As we cannot find evidence against evolution in verse 9, neither can we take "A king is not saved by his great army; a warrior is not delivered by his great strength," or "The war horse is a vain hope for victory," to mean that such means are unimportant (armies, force, heroes, horses) because God only has to speak and, behold, He promptly gives victory without all this. Here again, the meaning is not that our trust in such things is put to shame, or that distrust is urged on us in matters of force and might, but rather that God's faithfulness must penetrate all of this. If His word doesn't accompany our words, then certainly these are but a vapor (Ps. 127:1).

In a text we considered before, God's faithfulness comes out most strikingly not when we only hear that something happens immediately after He has spoken, but when we hear that it has already happened *before* He has spoken it. Recall how "he who sat upon the throne" says to John, "Write this, for these words are trustworthy and true. . . . It is done!" (Rev. 21:5-6). His word is so much a deed that His deeds do not come running after (as is the case with us), but the words come after the deeds! That's how true is God's speaking and how faithful is His word. This can help us in our systematic theology. We come to grips here with an important idea—that of the counsel of God. This doesn't function apart from history as though it were a decision taken from eternity and lying before all our days. It functions as God's faithfulness that accompanies us all through all of the world's weal and woe and—what is more—breaks through and negates our unfaithfulness. In theological terminology it might be well to substitute the "faithfulness" for the "counsel" of God, if only to avoid misunderstanding.

Let no one say that our concern here is with the word of God rather than with His faithfulness. The two are one in this Psalm and everywhere in the Bible. We only have to observe what the word does when it "becomes flesh." The Bible teaches that this results in one great demonstration of faithfulness to men (Heb. 2:14-18). And not only to men. The whole creation comes to rest when He speaks His word of might (Matt. 8:26). It is His faithfulness to creation that makes Jesus speak the redeeming word.

Word or Spirit?

Our text not only speaks about the word by which the heavens were made. We read also: "and all their host" (which actually means the same) are made "by the breath of his mouth." To whom or what is all this attributed—to the word or to the breath of God, to word or to Spirit?

Pointing to Psalm 31:5, N. H. Ridderbos observes that for the Israelite "the breath of the mouth of the Lord" and "the Spirit of the Lord" are "fluid conceptions that merge into one another," and also that the distinction between word and Spirit is very slight indeed.

He adds that this distinction is "yet" very slight. Certainly our trinitarian confession depends more on the New Testament than on the Old. Yet even in the New we come back to "Now the Lord is the Spirit" (2 Cor. 3:17). That is to say, we must not be too concerned about making a distinction in our text. It's obviously impossible to think of one without the other.

No. We cannot think of the Spirit without thinking of Him who has said, "he will take what is mine" (John 16:14), just as, to turn it around, the word is inconceivable without the conception by the Holy Spirit (Luke 1:35). The church is unthinkable apart from Him to whom all authority in heaven and on earth is given (Matt. 28:18). Nor can we think of the church apart from Him who opened Lydia's heart to the word (Acts 16:14). Thus far we have "only" spoken of the church, of the works of redemption. However, our Psalm bears witness that word and Spirit work together not only in the works of redemption but also in those of creation. Ultimately they do nothing more and want nothing more than this when redemption is no longer needed and when once again creation can be left to itself in the most marvelous evolution we'll ever know. As we step out of the church and into the world of nature and culture already we throw ourselves into this work —and not in any mood of despair! All this belongs to things which, so far as the word or faithfulness of God is concerned, not only *must* still happen (Rev. 22:6) but *have* already happened (Rev. 21:6). The Spirit and the bride summon us to this, for they vie with each other as they call to us "Come"! (Rev. 22:17).

AND YET

> *"Many are the afflictions of the righteous;*
> *but the Lord delivers him out of them all."*
>
> —Psalm 34:19

To be quite honest, this kind of text irritates us—and not just a little! That goes for the second part as well as for the first. We don't *want* to believe the first, and we *can't* believe the second.

An irritating sound

We don't want to get used to the idea of life's wretchedness. Especially as "righteous," we don't want to do this. As believers, as church members who work at it, as Christians—we had secretly thought we would be more pampered. We don't think the two really belong together—a Christian life and a wretched life. We don't think it ought to be this way. What particularly irritates us is that here it's not wretchedness in general to which reference is made but to very many miseries. It makes us think not of one, two, three (or more) big blows that may strike a person during his life, but of the endless goings-on, knocking about, fretting, and complaining of every day. Isn't it the latter that are so desperately hard to reconcile with the life of faith? That's the first part.

And then, just when we've gotten a little older and learned to compose ourselves and to put up with this or that, as good or bad as it may be, there's the second part of our text in which we hear that we're going to be delivered out of all the things described above! That too can irritate us terribly. Precisely because we're "righteous," believers, church members who work at it, we think this happens to us all too seldom. After the first part, we say, "How am I doing now?" We refuse to see the first, and we find it hard to get a right view of the second. Precisely because we're "righteous," we don't understand the wretchedness, supposing it much too bad. And precisely because we're "righteous," we don't understand the deliverances, supposing these much too good. The necessity of the first eludes us, and the comfort of the second eludes us. How irritating!

Shame and comfort

Perhaps we can learn something about our irritation—about shame and trust—from One who is presented to us as example time and again. Let's consider this.

How many calamities struck Him! How many calamities described in the Psalms struck Him, can be applied to Him, were literally branded on His body, culminating in that dreadful cry, "My God, my God, why hast thou forsaken me?" (Ps. 22:1; Matt. 27:46)! What calamities of ours or of our world was He spared? Doesn't the prophet say that the Lord put on Him all our afflictions, our diseases, and the greatest castastrophe, sin (Isa. 53:4-6)? Are there any temptations He did not know? In the Epistle to the Hebrews I read that He was "in every respect . . . tempted as we are" (Heb. 4:15). We can fill this in! The Epistle adds, "yet without sinning." Despite everything He remained righteous. What a combination of trouble and righteousness! He had reason enough to be divinely irritated but—and here's the point—*He* was not. He was one "who, though he was in the form of God, did not count equality with God a thing to be grasped, but emptied himself, taking the form of a servant, being born in the likeness of men. And being found in human form he humbled himself and became obedient unto death, even death on a cross" (Phil. 2:6-8). How this combination of wretchedness and righteousness puts our irritation to shame!

But how comforting! Look how He was delivered. The rest of our text ("He keeps all his bones; not one of them is broken") is specifically applied to Him (John 19:36). To be sure, the circumstances and the fulfillment are different, for the Psalmist was surely thinking of this life. Imagine an accident, with people running to it and everyone thinking, "He's in a bad way!" But look, he's all right and even walks away unhurt. He can rejoice, and we with him. That's what the poet meant. It was different with Jesus. He was "not all right" for He was dead, really dead. But look again a little later and see Him appear—and in what manner! Bones not broken don't compare with this resurrection from the dead or with this glorified body with which He ascends to heaven and sits at the right hand of God. Our poet had no idea of this!

Irritation forbidden

This example of shame and comfort, of lesson and promise, given us in the tormented and righteous one, Jesus Christ, holds a mandate for us. For one thing, we should not be so surprised or terribly vexed when calamities overtake us. This applies not only to those that come to us in common with everyone else, but especially to those that come to us because we're believers. It could be argued that life in general is wretched but that, on top of all this, Christian life is extra wretched. ". . . a servant is not greater than his master" (John 13:16), and "If they persecuted me, they will persecute you," as Jesus said (John 15:20). The persecution need not be by lion claws or SS boots or blank bullets or brainwashing. It need not take place in the arena, by the Gestapo, by racial discrimination, or by a people's commissar. It can also happen at home, at the office, or on a train. What can happen? That people simply can't stomach us because we're Christians—that they're annoyed and nettled and distant. On our part we must not be annoyed by this for we've been told what to expect (John 16:1-4). We should have known all along what to expect.

It's not easy for a Christian to overcome this annoyance, especially when faced with the extra wretchedness. Moreover, it's a dead serious matter because annoyance can become denial before

I realize it. Look at Peter. Happily that story teaches us not only
that one who doesn't take offense in Christ is blessed (Matt. 11:6)
but that one who has done so and weeps bitterly over it is also
blessed (Matt. 26:75; John 21:17).

Worth a poem

Actually, we're already in the second part of our study which is
concerned with the second half of our text. We need to believe
more in deliverance. To begin, we must not say it's typically Old
Testament to do this. While the Old Testament is acquainted with
very optimistic sounds (Ps. 37:25), it's also acquainted with very
pessimistic sounds which are at loggerheads with the first part of
the text. Just as we must not dream back to the Old Testament as
though deliverance then went smoothly, we should not dream forward to the New Jerusalem, supposing that only then will our text
find fulfillment. The text wants to be experienced in the present,
and so do its deliverances—a thousandfold. How could the poet
see or do this? Well, he did not know about *that* one resurrection,
but he did know of many others. I think it went something like
this: a man had been sick and had experienced it as calamity because it had taken him away from his work and cost him much
pain—had almost cost him his faith. Perhaps he had even
thought, "This is it." But look, he recovered! The poet had known
many such situations in his own life, catastrophic situations, as
well as many calamities that especially harassed him as a believer.
(For that matter, can't it be argued that believers have a harder
time with sickness, death, and pain than do others?) But look
how often things have turned out well. Thinking about all this, he
thought it deserved a poem. The Psalmists wrote their Psalms
about such things. They let the troubles come out of the wains-
coating, but also the deliverances—every time again. Every day
had enough of its own evil, but also of its own goal. If we would
only let this come home sufficiently to us every day we would
then be able to say more and even think of the hereafter and of
the truly royal way in which the words "the LORD delivers him
out of them all" will then hold good.

And yet

Perhaps the text does make for irritation—but it doesn't need to. It ought to make for seriousness and joy. That *must* be possible. Especially if we put the second part after the first, it will also mean that we shall not be tempted beyond what we can bear, as Paul says (1 Cor. 10:13). The text means "and yet." This paradox is present not only in the New Testament but in the Old. Look at the difference between verse 18, where we hear of a broken heart, and verse 20, where we hear that a broken heart is out of the question. For us this "and yet" is never seen with greater power than at Golgotha. What a death *and yet* what a life! The most catastrophic event of history has become the sign of a deliverance without equal. Whoever has seen the very worst Friday of history become Good Friday will believe that everything is possible, including our text, and will believe more than the poet could possibly have believed before Golgotha. Shame on us that, after Golgotha, we often believe less than he!

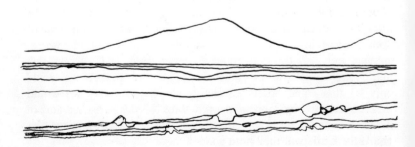

THE THIRD KIND

"Bestir thyself, and awake for my right,
for my cause, my God and my Lord!
Vindicate me, O Lord, my God,
according to thy righteousness . . ."

—Psalm 35:23-24

According to this Psalm there are two kinds of believers, both of whom are at fault.

The first kind

The first kind is the permanent Pharisee. He likes to talk only about his own rights and his own righteousness. We must not suppose this makes him unbearable in everyone's eyes. That need not be the case. Under this kind we might meet the smartest and most gifted business men—though at the same time they may be the most hardboiled. They can also cut a good figure in politics, especially in foreign affairs—especially insofar as this can still be called Realpolitik. They can even do this as Christians and as church members. It's typical of them that they never have any questions about their own Christianity or about the rightness of their church.

The second kind

The second kind is the permanent tax collector. He doesn't want to hear anything about his own rights or righteousness. He thinks a Christian really ought not hold on to any rights. He wants to talk only about the righteousness of God. If that's the way he looks at his personal life, it's certainly also the way he regards political and social life. If the first kind never questions the value of social and political life, the second does nothing but question it. In view of God's righteousness, the difference between earthly justice and injustice is largely lost for him. In this darkness all cats are gray. If the first kind is a Calvinist caricature, the second is a Lutheran caricature.

The third kind

The third kind, with which this Psalm is concerned, is the kind of believer who is not embarrassed to talk about his own right and righteousness, to believe in this and fight for it, and isn't even embarrassed to let God fight for it. The whole Psalm could be described as being occasioned by one's own right and righteousness, culminating in such expression as "awake for my right."

It's possible to describe the Psalm this way. But, with just as good reason, it's possible to describe the Psalm as occasioned by God's righteousness, culminating in the words, "Vindicate me, O LORD, my God, according to thy righteousness." The same comes into view at the Psalm's close where the poet first says, "Let those who desire my vindication shout for joy and be glad," and then adds, "Great is the LORD"! Apparently, as in Psalm 127, one doesn't exclude the other. A man's own struggle and zeal for his cause don't exclude the divine struggle. In the Psalms believers may look like Pharisees in their doing and not doing, but they're not Pharisees. Their "pharisaical" doing and not doing doesn't keep them from concluding, like Paul, "Let him who boasts, boast in the Lord"—which must not be called a typical New Testament wisdom, for we meet it explicitly not only in 1 Corinthians 1:31 but also in Jeremiah 9:24.

To turn it around, for such a man God's righteousness doesn't exclude his own righteousness. The fact that God must build and preserve the city doesn't alter the fact that there must be builders and soldiers.

Perhaps we have not noticed sufficiently that by God's righteousness we should not limit our understanding of this to its deepest manifestation: the justification of the ungodly (Rom. 4:5). The trouble with the Pharisee apparently is that he's never heard of that. The trouble with the tax collector apparently is that he's never heard anything else. God's righteousness is not exhausted in forgiveness. He also wants to bring grist to the mill.

Requiting good for evil

Biblically speaking, if we don't want to experience a complete separation of God's righteousness from our own or cling one-sidedly to either, this assumes a good deal. If anyone sees his own righteousness linked with God's, he must be able to say with the Psalmist that he and his cause are hated "without cause." This comes out twice in verse 7 and is repeated in verse 19. In verse 15 we meet the same kind of astonishment over so much evil against one who means so well and who knows how to act accordingly. There the poet speaks of the pugnacity of those "whom I knew not." Why did they make life so difficult for him? That says a good deal. All the more so—and compared with this positive note the preceding, no matter how convincing, sounds almost negative—because he himself had only requited evil with good. Listen to him. "But I, when they were sick—I wore sackcloth, I afflicted myself with fasting, I prayed with my head bowed on my bosom, as though I grieved for my friend or my brother; I went about as one who laments his mother, bowed down and in mourning. But at my stumbling . . ."

Is there really a third kind?

If we apply a little self-analysis to our own crises—whether crises in marriage, in labor, with children, between nations, between churches—we're not inclined to appeal too quickly to our own right and righteousness. How often have I and my point of view, my party, my church, and my nation not been hated *with* cause? And, even if I haven't been responsible for this, to what extent have I requited evil with good and heaped coals of fire on

my enemy's head, as the whole Bible tells me to do, from this
Psalm on to Romans 12? Might not the second kind of person be
right after all? Is there really a third kind?

Going on stubbornly

The tax collector is always right over against the Pharisee, but
we can't split Christendom into sheer Pharisees and sheer tax
collectors. After all, there's also the believer of this Psalm and he
doesn't give the impression that he thinks himself alone. He's certainly not that kind of Pharisee! We must go on stubbornly beyond
people who are concerned only with their own righteousness
(even if we are these people) by remembering God's righteousness and that earth cannot exist apart from heaven. However, just
as stubbornly must we go on beyond people concerned only with
God's righteousness (even if we are these people) by remembering our own righteousness and that heaven doesn't exist apart
from earth. Thus something like a third kind of believer must
arise, the kind that populates the world of the Psalms. And is this
world really different from ours?

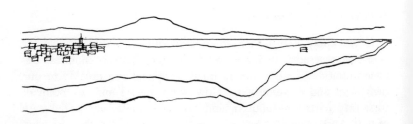

GOD AND LIGHT

*"For with thee is the fountain of life;
in thy light do we see light."*

—Psalm 36:9

There is light and there is light. We could write the first with a
capital letter and the second with a small letter. There is God—
and there is the sun. Let's not limit light to what literally gives
light, for that would not be an adequate exegesis of the little word
"light" as it appears in the Psalms. Light stands for everything that
makes life bright and glad and happy. It makes us think not only
of the sun but also of health, of music and lovely words, of land-
scapes and living rooms, of the wonders of technology—in short,
of everything that's worthwhile. There is God—and there is life.
By the latter the Psalm thinks not only of people but of animals.
In the world of the Psalms things and plants are also part of it.
There is life and there is life.

Light and life

And yet, we haven't said enough when we write the first with a
capital letter and the second with a small letter. Doing that might
still suggest that they belong to the same common denominator,
light and life, in which both God and man participate. But that's
not the way it is. God is greater than "the" light or "the" life.
Immediately preceding our verse and in the same text we read:

"For with thee is the fountain of life." God is something other than life itself. He is the fountain of life, the source of life. He is life in such fashion that we have no conception of it—save only through Jesus Christ, who is constantly called light and life—and with reason. But just when we've met Him, we discover to our astonishment that we are something quite other than God. To mix this up and see it differently is to look at it like Adam, to see it wrongly (Gen. 3:5-6).

This is important because it leads us to say two things. God is much more than life for He is the source of life. We can add that He is "only" the source of life. This is not to point to some kind of powerlessness of God but rather to His power. There's an inseparable connection. He wants us to see this wealth of light and life not as though it were only a part of Himself but as something independent, as something apart from Himself. He gives us light for our eyes—and much more. He was pleased to create us, to place us outside Himself. That's what gives our light and life significance!

What of Psalm verses like: *God* "is my light and my salvation; whom shall I fear (Ps. 27:1)? True enough, but the second part of the verse shows that the poet doesn't see a way out. When he thinks of light and life, he *must* fall back on God, else he wouldn't have life anymore. On the other hand, we must not do this so quickly and arbitrarily as to assume that actually only God is, as though creation (with all this offers in light and energy) disappears in *that* light. Anyone who tries to skip over all this on his way to God will not reach God but only an abstraction—and that will be his rightful judgment. We may disclose ourselves this way but we do God no service, for He has recognized all sorts of light and life outside Himself. After all, He created them!

A person may be sick, lying alone in a hospital, vainly gasping for light and life, simply because he or she is thinking only of God and not of nurses' help, of how much worse it might have been, of a friendly neighbor, of flowers on the table, of an exhilarating book, of the good words of many good friends. Light and life in abundance!

In or by

Our translation reads: "in thy light do we see light." We can also read it: "by thy light do we see light." J. Ridderbos prefers the latter translation. He sees the preposition "by" pointing to the "ground" of our light. The word "fountain" (Dutch: "source"), which occurs in the same text, supports this interpretation. This leads us to the thought that we have to thank the life and light that is in God for all the life and light there is in the world. The meaning of everything that gladdens our heart makes us look behind us and above us to its source. That becomes the occasion for a song of thanksgiving.

If we began by accenting the *independence* of life (as it's intended because it's created), we must now accent its *dependence*. This comes out much less strongly in the preposition "by" than "in." The former could lead us to deism which taught that God made the world as a watchmaker starts a watch running and then lets it out of his hands so that the thing runs by itself. God is supposed to have let the creation out of His hands after creating it, and now we'll have to sort it out by ourselves.

There's a great deal of truth in this accent on independence. There's also a great deal of error in it because it lacks mercy. As if creating were not also preserving and, if necessary, redeeming!

We'll speak of redeeming presently. First we must speak of preserving. The light of God not only lies behind us and above us; it encircles us also from "behind and before" (Ps. 139:5). It not only leads us to thanksgiving but to knowledge. It's not enough to give thanks for it. We can also do something with it! ". . . in thy light do we see light" has tremendous implications. In the light of His word (Ps. 119:105) we understand more about all the light and life around us. The Christian organizations of our land— school, university, radio, labor union, political party—can be seen as a legitimate exegesis of our text. We must not be afraid to look at it this way. We ought to be glad it's this way.

We can return to our preposition in two ways. Both "by" and "in" are meaningful. It makes no sense to put them over against one another in the practice of sanctification. It only makes sense to keep them together. Without "in," "by" becomes deism and positivism, no matter how grateful. Without "by," "in" becomes pietism and quietism, no matter how pious.

The dark is light enough

The foregoing discussion is rather theoretical compared to the practical concern of the Psalm. Actually, who are the "we" referred to in our text? "We" are the "oppressed faithful," says J. Ridderbos, "the poet and his companions." Accordingly, they are not folks who joyously recount all that life has to offer of light. On the contrary. Apparently life has nothing more to offer them. Nothing is left them except to fall back on God and discover that, if nothing is left them and if creation has left them in the lurch, still He is never an abstraction but the purest light and purest life. Could it be that this says something not only about the address of the faithful but also about the address of the wicked? Just as the former can still find God in nothing, the latter can't find Him in everything. Seldom have we seen these verses so beautifully portrayed for the faithful as in the closing verses of the prophet Habakkuk, where the "yet" of the Lord is able to turn "nothing" into "everything."

So much for the Old Testament. As for the New Testament, we think of the way this verse is fulfilled in those two men walking to Emmaus, completely disillusioned and defeated. Life had nothing left for them. It was dead, for their God had died in three hours of thick darkness and was now hidden under the ground, gone. Then suddenly, that dark grave is bordered with white lightning and a radiant appearance encounters them. He came to them with so much light and life that, as they were at table with Him, they didn't just become lighter of heart. We read that their hearts *burned* within them (Luke 24:1-32)!

THE WICKED SHALL PERISH

". . . their sword shall enter their own heart . . ."

—Psalm 37:15

Who would plunge a sword into his own heart? The wicked. There will be an end to the wicked. That is to say, there will be an end to those who continue and can't stop—the Psalm gives an accurate description—hatching evil plans, falling upon the wretched and the poor, slaughtering the upright, heaping up godless riches, taking without giving, preying upon the righteous. In short, there will be an end to the "luxurious parasites" of mankind. There will be an end to the ruthless oppressors of all times, classes, and nations. Of course. If the wicked don't eventually perish, then *the others* will perish eventually and never be able to "possess the land," as the Psalm promises.

Who are the others?

Who are the "others"? We know well enough who or what the wicked are. But the others? Are they those who are not wicked? That's putting it negatively. The others are not simply those who are not wicked, not oppressors, etc. They are the humble (verse 11) or, as we usually say, the meek. But, in the Bible and in our Psalm, the meek are not simply those who don't participate in the shameful deeds described above. They are those who know how to oppose all this. They are not only strong in "avoidance of

evil," but also in the "doing of good" (vs. 27). We might compare them with those whom we called "good Hollanders" during
the war. These were not Hollanders who didn't go along in perse-
cuting Jews. These were the Hollanders who went out to hide
Jews. In the Sermon on the Mount the meek are on a par with
those who hunger and thirst after righteousness, with the peacemakers, with the merciful. One is the same as the other. They're
conspicuous not only because they are victims but because they
do the opposite of victimizing.

Only these, the meek, may say what is said here: "their sword
shall enter their own heart," the wicked will perish. Only on their
lips will this not sound cruel or rancorous, but right and even
merciful. That's why only the most meek of all, God, can say it
perfectly—pronounce judgment on someone and utter this danger-
ous text.

It may take a long time

Someone might observe that it may take a long time before the
contemptible deeds and their spokesmen will disappear from the
face of the earth.

That may be, but it's not altogether true. We Hollanders found
it was a fairly short time, 1940-1945, that injustice in our midst
was calling the tune. That was long enough, but comparatively
speaking, in view of the history of injustice in the world, we
should not complain. If one observes carefully, he perceives that
the Psalms swarm with occasions where we hear that the wicked
have perished and that the meek have again come into their own.
This is noted carefully each time for it would be considered
shameful ingratitude to neglect it. To be sure, our forefathers used
to exaggerate this by supposing the finger of God was always
working in their favor, and we don't need to go back very far to
see this. On many Anglo-Saxon war monuments one can find the
words that the fallen died for their land and for God. The self-evident character of this escapes us, for example, in the Boer War.
Moreover, we younger folk don't understand how older folk, in a

political victory of the orthodox Protestant party under Colijn, could sing:

> Let God arise, and scattered
> let all his en'mies be;
> And let all those that do him hate
> before his presence flee.

We used to exaggerate our thanksgiving, and that easily becomes pharisaism. But would we not go to the other extreme if we no longer want any monuments of thanksgiving erected when once again a stop has been put to some shameful injustice in the world?

It can also happen in reverse. It often happens that monuments of dictatorship have been erected, and a man may have to wait a long time for these to fall into ruin. We don't need to tell the Psalmists this. They had a "bellyful" of it! But that's not the concern here. Here we're concerned with the opposite, with what should not be erased but carefully preserved. That must be the meaning of that strangely optimistic verse 25 in our Psalm: "I have been young, and now am old; yet I have not seen the righteous forsaken or his children begging bread." I'm sure that in the history of the church many righteous have experienced the opposite—an enormous amount of forsakenness and hunger for themselves and for their children. I don't think our poet would deny or be unaware of this. He only meant to say that *he,* thank God, didn't have to experience it. For him this is so extraordinary and moving that he promptly preserves it in this verse. That's what makes this verse not strangely *optimistic* but (and that's not the same thing!) strangely thankful.

It may take only a short while that oppression calls the tune and that the wicked do what they want. Granted—but it can also take a long time. It's possible to read something quick, but also to read something overpowering, into the image of the luxurious parasite plant. The Nazi hydra may have harassed us for five years, but across the border people had trouble with it much longer. And for seven million Jews it took so long for the end of the dictator that it took *too* long. And not only for them. The fact remains that the judgment about which our text speaks can come late, very late, so late that we must begin to speak of the last judgment. That the Jew in our Psalm reckoned with something like this and *had* to reckon with it is evident from the fact that, now and then, he speaks not of himself but of his descendants. The "now" inevitably becomes "then."

Indeed, it can take a long time, a very long time, much too long for us to see it. We think again of those seven million Jews, and we also think of One in particular who was so pressed that He cried, "My God, my God, why hast thou forsaken me?" (Matt. 27:46). But we must not blot out what happened there—a resurrection, and this not primarily for Himself or even by Himself, but primarily for those for whom it took too long for the wicked to perish and for our text to be fulfilled.

With expectation beats our heart

There's something we can expect from the meek, particularly from the meek—namely, patience. Similarly, we can expect something from the wicked even if they're really wicked—namely, conversion! Not only the New Testament knows this hope (2 Peter 3:9), but also the Old Testament (Ezek. 18:21-28). Of course, this is bound up with the unheard-of patience of One who is most meek, the Lord God Himself, who has known how to express this patience through the ages (they really exist on it). We may always still expect this of Him.

But, doesn't God actually will the destruction of the wicked? No, of course not! We would want it. I think of the story of Jonah. God wills the opposite. I think of the story of Nineveh (happily the same story). We must read carefully. The text says that the wicked will fall upon *their own* swords, and that's not the same as God's sword. In any case, we may not identify the two. The judgment, including and especially the last judgment, is something we bring upon ourselves. In his commentary, N. H. Ridderbos writes: "In powerful manner it is made clear that the wicked have only themselves to blame for the calamity they have received." Significantly, even Article 16 of the Netherland Confession of Faith—an article which could lead to misunderstanding about predestination by suggesting arbitrariness if we didn't link it immediately with Article 20 and with Sunday 31 of the Heidelberg Catechism—is concerned with a fall in which man "has cast himself" and therefore not God!

If someone, frightened by Psalm 37:15, should object: "But surely, the wicked *ought not* to perish in their wickedness, they *ought not* to fall on their own sword. Can they not repent?"— then the answer is: "*Of course* they ought not to fall on their own sword, and *or course* they can repent. What prevents them?" This is the joyful message of the gospel: nothing and no one prevents them from repenting of their abundance of pride. Or perhaps one thing: a lack of meekness on the part of the others?

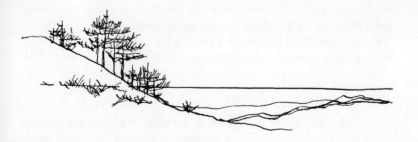

A SONG OF LONGING

"Lord, all my longing is known to thee . . ."

—Psalm 38:9

When we see a person cry, we go to him and ask anxiously: "What happened? What's going on? What have they done to you? What do you want? What have you lost? How can we help?" Isn't that why a great many people cry? Someone has done something to them, has caused them grief. And yet—strangely enough, since it doesn't happen very often—suddenly there's a person crying, not because someone has caused him grief but because he has caused grief. Not because he wants something but because he wants to be rid of something. Peter is such a man. At a given moment we could have found him and seen that he "wept bitterly" (Matt. 26:75). That was a strange crying spell, one you don't meet often. He wept, not because someone had done something to him, but because he had done something to God. There's something humilitating and sobering about this crying, an appeal. Not to ignore other crying but rather, in the midst of all sorts of sorrow, not forget *this* sorrow—sorrow not because someone has done something to us but because we have done something to God. This will soothe all that other sorrow a bit and, what is so needed, bring it back into proper perspective.

When we see someone longing

It's like that when we speak of longing. What do we usually think of? There are too many to name. The song of longing is al-

ready very old, as old as the history of the world and as old as
the story of our life. We never stop longing. As children we were
always longing for some sweets. Actually, we still do, but now the
sweets are more sophisticated. Sometimes—and these may be our
best moments—we don't even know exactly what we desire. A
person may stand dreaming before a sunset, or he may dream
while listening to a good jazz record that pours out music that
"puts into words" things that can't be put into words.

Perhaps this has been drawn somewhat egocentrically. Dreamers easily become egocentric. Greshoff shook himself awake in
1936 with his poem, "I beat the drums and drum the dreamers
awake." He wanted to ban a great many longings of his day as
luxury. After all, those were the days—the poet realized this
sooner and better than did the politicians—when the Nazi beast
was rising, days when a man should have had only one longing:
that has to go. Greshoff longed for righteousness more than for
beauty.

The poet of our Psalm goes even further. To be sure, Greshoff
longed to be delivered from unrighteousness—and that's splendid.
But he longed primarily to be delivered from the unrighteousness
of *others,* while the Psalmist longs primarily to be delivered from
his *own* unrighteousness. That's what disturbs him so much.

Sick of sin

That might be the explanation of his "sickness." Generally
speaking, it's difficult to know exactly what to make of the many
sicknesses in the Psalms. Should we take them literally and physically, or figuratively and spiritually? In this case it doesn't seem
too difficult. Birkeland, who finds only three Psalms as actual
sickness-Psalms, counts this one among them. Besides, in this
Psalm there's something else. This sickness is the result of sin, a
link which doesn't occur often, at least not so directly. But it does
occur. I can invite my own calamities. It's to his credit that the
poet applies to himself this infrequent link. He makes his sick-
ness-Psalm not a Psalm of lamentation but a penitential Psalm.
It's to the poet's credit that he sees sin in his sickness.

Personally, I think this isn't the most obvious explanation. Undoubtedly the Psalm points to sickness, but in such an alarming and extreme manner that I can't take it literally. I find it difficult simply to combine an exclusively bodily fright with what I read here: "all the day I go about mourning." Bedridden would be easier. It seems to me that we must take this figuratively without minimizing any of the gravity of the situation. Quite the contrary! The poet views himself as sick of sin. He finds that he "stinks" of sin, and he's completely sick with longing to be rid of this sin.

Greater than Solomon

I hope no one will say, "How romantic and melodramatic that sounds!" or "Isn't this pure nonsense?" The opposite is more likely to be true. Every longing not acquainted with *this* longing is pure romance and pure melodrama! Compared with our longings before a beautiful sunset or jazz score, the longing of this one man is as sobering as that crying spell of Peter—and it can sober us amid our own outbursts of grief. That's not nonsense and certainly not religious nonsense. The poet is not a neurotic. He doesn't revel in his consciousness of sin and in his longing for forgiveness. In verse 20, he still seems to have quite a bit to "offer" in the midst of the enmity he must undergo in his misery (for where there's sorrow there is also pleasure in this sorrow by others). Over against a lot of evil that he has to undergo he can still point to a lot of good. Like Peter who said, "Lord, you know everything; you know that I love you" (John 21:17), he still has something to offer even though he sees to it that he doesn't conclude his lament with this. He doesn't end with an appeal to himself but with an appeal to God. "Make haste to help me, O Lord, my salvation!"

We might almost say, "A greater than Solomon is here too!" What did Solomon ask for? He didn't ask first of all for riches or a long life or many victories. He longed for an understanding heart (1 Kings 3:11-12, K.J.V.). The Psalmist thrusts deeper still and asks for a *small* heart (though ultimately that's the same thing).

Seek first . . .

Where do we meet God first and most often? In our longing to be rid of sorrow or in our longing for forgiveness from the consciousness of sin? That's where we meet God first and most often because that's where we meet Him with greatest longing. Truly, man can be characterized by the word "longing." But God can be characterized by the same word much more. Anyone who knows Jesus Christ a little will agree. What longing? "I have earnestly desired to eat this passover with you" (Luke 22:15). That is to say, I have earnestly desired to share your deepest sorrow.

A thousand and one longings have to do with the Kingdom of God. The childlike longing for sweets belongs to it, and the older boy's longing for a girl belongs to it (Eccles. 11:9). The sunset and the world of music and lovely words belong to it. All this belongs to it for the Kingdom of God is not embarrassed by all sorts of childlikeness and all sorts of emotion (just name them)!—but *this* comes first. Then the rest will be added to us (Matt. 6:33). And what is true of the New Testament is true of the Old Testament. When Solomon asked first of all for an understanding heart, God said that He would also give him riches and a long life and many victories. In the preceding Psalm we read, "Take delight in the LORD, *and* he will give you the desires of your heart" (Ps. 37:4). That's the legitimate order of our longings, not the other way round. The man who simply lets himself be absorbed by desires will discover that they choke him (Mark 4:19). That's a grim reminder from the parable of the seed that was choked by the thorns of many desires. That warning is exceeded by the grim reminder we meet in Psalm 106:14-15 where I hear that a man, even a whole nation, even the best nation, can have such "wanton craving" that what was written next was fulfilled: "he gave them what they asked, but sent a wasting disease among them." The two can go together. How terrible!

Whoever follows the right prescription, however, is "made to measure" so that he can reach the fulfilling of all his desires. It's not that he becomes tall enough to reach it, for adulthood is but a poor guarantee in this sort of thing. No, it's because at last he's *small* enough to reach and to attain it (Matt. 18:3).

Longing for God

In the deepest sense, all longing is longing for God. That's why our longing never ends, and why it cannot be circumscribed—because God can't be circumscribed. Augustine was right: "Restless is our heart until it finds its rest in God." However, if God has one beginning—to put it a bit strangely—then He begins where the poet began, with forgiveness and the desire for it. That's where He begins. But then afterward there's no end to the road. Certainly there's much groaning in the Psalms but afterward—and perhaps, yes, because of it—even "the floods clap their hands" (Ps. 98:8)!

A VERY GLOOMY SOUND

*"Look away from me, that I may know gladness,
before I depart and be no more!"*

—Psalm 39:13

In this Psalm again we meet someone in great difficulties. How did it happen? Do enemies play a part? Could it be that notorious enemy called illness? Or is it the nagging thought that life without God and neighbor seems to be so much easier and rewarding and happy than the life of a believer? Is he his own worst enemy? Is he at loggerheads with himself? Certainly, the last is true but, as is often the case, we can't be sure about the rest. The really difficult things have no name. A person doesn't know how to name or account for them. The story one could tell about such difficulties would take so long that he might as well not try. Who can tell me exactly why I find myself in the dumps?

Roaring billows

Whatever the case, the gloomy sounds of this Psalm leave no doubt that the difficulties are serious.

There are more of such ominous sounds. Psalm 73 is an example. However, in that Psalm the poet already has behind him what our poet must still combat, and that's quite a difference. There's a difference between seeing someone staggering to shore after barely having escaped drowning, dead tired but happy—and seeing someone fighting for his life in the raging billows of the sea. Moreover, what is still somewhat restrained in Psalm 73 here bursts out in our Psalm. Here life is all struggle and we don't hear anything about victory. The happy ending usually included at the close of a Psalm is not mentioned. If we examine the last lines, the opposite seems to be the case—for these lines sound the most somber because the most resigned. In short, this Psalm has a very gloomy sound. To repeat, there are more Psalms like this one. Psalm 88 is an example. These happen to be the worst two!

Inappropriate?

It's so gloomy that some have suggested that it's simply not appropriate. The commentator Hengstenberg, for example, has trouble with verses 3-6, in which the poet certainly pours out his feelings in most dreadful manner. Calvin too thought David was going too far here. He has particular difficulty with the verse that sounds gloomiest to us, verse 13. Yet it's too bad that some view it this way. Let's be honest. The somber tone of this Psalm will be familiar to a great many readers, and no one will be stranger to it completely. That holds some comfort. It might be that what Calvin won't let us say even a single time, God lets us say time after time. It might be that God doesn't mind if we say what is uppermost on our hearts. Perhaps it was a "liberal" tendency in Calvin's exegesis that he took this passage as so human that it had to be removed from divine inspiration. As if the one excludes the other!

We can summarize by saying: well and good; it may be all right to talk this way at times. It may be some comfort, for who doesn't think of life so gloomily at times? But to say this isn't enough. I imagine someone would find this paltry comfort unless he knows what happened to the man in the Psalm. What did happen to him?

What happened?

Indeed. What did happen to him? Would God actually have turned His countenance away from him? That would have to be

God's angry countenance, since in the Bible the faithful always ask God to turn His friendly countenance *toward* them. We usually say, "Please smile, God!" Here, however, it is, "Please don't be so angry, God!"

Undoubtedly He has done just that. Even in Psalm 73, where —as we have to admit—while what can be called sinful is barely restrained, the poet closes by confessing: "Thou dost hold my right hand" (vs. 23). That's the point, someone may object. What's said in that Psalm is not said in Psalm 39.

Is that so? I hear several sounds that are anything but gloomy. The first is verse 7, where I hear: "And now, Lord, for what do I wait? My hope is in thee." That's no trifle. I've never found in the Bible that anyone's hope in God is put to shame. At first sight the second sound seems to contradict this, I find this in verse 12: "Hear my prayer, O LORD, and give ear to my cry; hold not thy peace at my tears! For I am thy passing guest, a sojourner, like all my fathers." Doesn't the poet kick himself deeper into the dumps with this last qualification?

No. What was life like for the stranger and sojourner in the world of the Bible? Good—indeed, very good. True, there were some restrictions: interest could be taken from the stranger but not from the fellow countryman (Deut. 23:20). For the rest, however, one must love him as though he were a fellow countryman (Lev. 19:33). He should feel more at home in Canaan than with his own people. We meet something similar in Psalm 84:10. There we meet one who "would rather be a doorkeeper in the house of my God" than to "dwell in the tents of wickedness." We could paraphrase this by saying: better a hard task with God than at ease with the wicked. Better to be with God with all my doubts than to be with the wicked with all my faith. Better a bit off the mark on God's side than completely at home with the wicked.

The same is true of the New Testament—indeed, more so! No longer is any difference drawn between the stranger and sojourner and God's chosen people. The *go'im* (Gentiles) belong to it (Eph. 2:14). According to Jesus—and He ought to know since He's at home with God—strangers and sojourners and those who hardly feel they belong do belong, not *perhaps* but *certainly*!

There's not a little peril someone might not feel this because he feels so dreadfully at home with God. We think of the Pharisee. And we also think of the tax collector who doesn't dare come farther than the threshold. We know what happened to both. It only "turned out well" for one, and that was the tax collector (Luke 18:14).

It turns out well

Of course, you must be able to feel a bit like the tax collector. The Psalmist can. His situation, no matter how miserable, doesn't lead him to sheer self-pity. Even though he can't avoid it altogether, and doesn't have to, and isn't expected to, this man is acquainted with the strange word of Lamentations: "Whoever complains, let him complain about his sins" (Lam. 3:39, Dutch). He feels very small and insignificant under the blows.

We would say: what would be easier for him than to escape into utter meaninglessness, feeling so insignificant and "nothing over against God"? We would say the man has every reason to let himself be prey to a feeling of tragedy. But that isn't the case. The last thing he says is not about tragedy but about guilt (vs. 11).

So it must have turned out all right for this man! With verse 13, we will not leave him behind and he will not leave us behind. Who else has said: "I will not leave you desolate" and "I go and prepare a place for you" (John 14:3, 18)? Jesus said that. He can prepare a place for us even if "I depart and be no more" (vs. 13). He can see to a "fourteenth" verse and happy ending, a gospel of the resurrection!

We must not say this too quickly. That is to say, we must not flee to heaven and the hereafter of the New Testament too quickly. If anyone is tempted to do so, the poet's voice, no matter how gloomy, is healthier. He wants God to stop looking angry *today*. He can't stand it one more day. And he's right. He should be congratulated, and that's why he isn't the sinner Calvin thought. Still, although this should not be put aside too easily and quickly for everyone, there still remains the final prospect—that at last I may "know gladness" and be "radiant" again, as the text actually says.

Warning and comfort

As gloomily as we began so radiantly we may conclude. It's like the Book of Revelation. There too we begin with stories of great oppressions and of those who had had to deal with blood (7:14). But we end differently, with a marriage of the Lamb (19:6-10). That seems to be very different, completely different. A gloomy beginning, a radiant conclusion—blood and betrothal! But is it so completely different? The Lamb doesn't think so. That sounds a great warning and also a great comfort.

THE BOOK OF GOD

"Then I said, 'Lo, I come;
in the roll of the book it is written for me.' "

—Psalm 40:7

A book, a book roll written about someone, in which a name (my name) appears, makes us think of something like predestination. That doesn't seem incorrect, and so we'll take it up once again—once again, since we've already done so in Psalm 30.

Not only a chair

I think it's not inaccurate to think of the book roll in terms of predestination.

But it makes quite a difference *how* we do this. It's true as long as I don't think one-sidedly about myself, of what happens to me. It's true if I also think of what happens through me. It's true if I don't think only of my own fate but also of the fate of others.

The Heidelberg Catechism (Question and Answer 66) tells us how we are to think of this.

There we read that I must do good works—i.e., to mean something for another and all that includes—not although I am redeemed, chosen, predestined to salvation, but *because* I am all this. Predestination is always predestination to good works (Eph. 2:10). I'm not redeemed, chosen, *period*; I'm redeemed, chosen *for*. Predestination is not only an armchair; it's a springboard. It will take us the rest of our lives to realize it is both—comfort and commission.

That's predestination

Accordingly, we can say that the roll of the book mentioned in the Psalm is no other than the book in which we're told what to do and not do—the law of God. It's not some other book! God's book and God's law occur together and in the same context in our Psalm (cf. vss. 7-8).

Whoever is curious about what's in the roll of the book gets to hear what he or she has to *do*. And then? We must bring a sacrifice. This isn't contradicted by verse 6: "Sacrifice and offering thou dost not desire . . . Burnt offering and sin offering thou hast not required." God would hardly command the bringing of sacrifices on one page and on the next withdraw or contradict this. The verses just quoted mean we must free the bringing of sacrifice from one-sidedness and ease. After all, we must first bring ourselves, else it's no use. What was the difference between Cain's sacrifice and Abel's? The difference didn't lie in the sacrifice. It lay in the heart behind the sacrifice. That is to say, if we're to do something for God, it's not something in general but what *we* have to do. Everyone can agree with this because it concerns *everyone*. That keeps it anonymous. What matters is what *I* have to do. That's why the poet says, "thy law is within my heart." That is to say, the law and I are one, of one mind.

To summarize, what does our book roll mean? It means something must be *done*. It means something must be done by *me*. The "open ear" mentioned in the preceding verse indicates obedience. Obedience, *my* obedience, is called for. That's what predestination means.

Henceforth that's the way I'll read my "roll of the book." That's the way I'll read the law. That's the way—it's all the same thing—I'll read the Bible. Now I know it's about *me*. It's also about Abraham, Isaac, and Jacob, etc., but especially it's about me and about what I must do about it. What matters is that I say, "Lo, I come"! It's like a mobilization order to which, as a good

soldier, I must answer gladly, quickly, and faithfully. That's what
predestination means.

We pause a moment over the striking word "then." "Then I
said, 'Lo, I come.' " To what does this refer? It can point to the
opened ear. When the poet received an open ear, *then* he obeyed.
That's the way J. Ridderbos takes it. N. H. Ridderbos prefers to
think of the familiar throne ascension theme in the Psalms. When
that had occurred and the poet had become king, *then* he said,
"Lo, I come." In that case the image of the soldier gives way to
the image of a king. There's something proud and festive in that
image. That too is what predestination means.

A sour business

If predestination means all this, then it takes some doing! And
this for two reasons.

First, because it's a sour business. The "roll of the book lies
upon me," so J. Ridderbos translates it. The writing is a prescription—and how! We could express the ambiguity of the text by
reading, "it oppresses me." Look at verse 4: it calls me away
from the fellowship of the proud and from those who "turn aside
to lies" (K.J.V.). But that's just the fellowship I seek and enjoy!
Nor do we gain popularity by it, if I understand verse 14 rightly.
Poverty and distress—whether understood literally or figuratively
doesn't matter, for in the Bible one is no less serious than the
other—are often my lot (vs. 17), at least if I'm obedient. Perhaps the extent to which poverty and distress (literally or figuratively) are my lot is the extent to which I am obedient! No, the
life of a believer is much harder than we expected. It's a sour
business.

It's so sour—and this is the second reason—that it often mis-
fires and seems to play havoc with my predestination. Listen to
the poet in verse 12. Countless miseries not only surround him
but seem to be occasioned by iniquities more numerous than the
hairs of his head. And the man who says this is the same man
who had said eight verses earlier: "Blessed is the man who makes

the LORD his trust"! That's the way the believer talks on Sunday
—but you should hear him on Monday! It's hard to believe that
the man of verse 12 is the same man who says in verse 7, "Lo, I
come."

In the roll of the book it is written of Me

We don't manage too well with our predestination, our commission, no matter how proud and festive. The poet knows that well
enough. He is a man, as we see from the first four verses, who
has been pulled "out of the drain" and for whom little is left save
an appeal for God's mercy (vs. 11). Fortunately he knows that
this is more than a *concept* but includes a whole *history,* the history of "wondrous deeds" that are more than can be numbered
(vs. 5). We know the last wonder (Heb. 1:1-2) of this history. In
the Bible, a wonder is always a miracle of mercy, and the greatest
wonder is Jesus Christ. At last we are where we need to be. For
the roll of the book was also written about *Him.* The law and the
Bible are also about Him! How indignantly He bursts out against
those travelers to Emmaus: "O foolish men and slow of heart:
that you did not recognize me in the Bible!" (Luke 24:25f). The
writer of the Epistle to the Hebrews even applied the whole text
to Jesus when he doesn't simply let a poet or someone else say it,
but Jesus: "Then I said, 'Lo, I have come to do thy will,
O God,' as it is written of me in the roll of the book" (Heb. 10:7).
In other words, when we say so proudly and confidently "Here
am I, Lord!" on Sunday, or at Christmas, or at our first profession
of faith, at some peak of faith—only to acknowledge in faith's
miry bog on Monday, "I'm no longer anywhere!"—then Jesus
says: "But I'm still here" (in the miry bog, etc.)!

Speaking of sour, *He* had it sour. I think of Gethsemane and
the prayer, "My Father, if it be possible, let this cup pass from
me" (Matt. 26:39). If ever a separation between sacrifice and
sacrificer were impossible, it's here. He was himself the sacrifice,
the slain Lamb par excellence. And he managed it! His sacrifice
—Golgotha—counted! How it counted! It even counted for the

whole world (1 John 2:2). That's why the Epistle to the Hebrews calls it unique (10:12).

Gift and task

But what if even after his coming and after Golgotha things still go wrong for the life of a believer? Indeed, things often do go wrong still. Not always, of course. There's also hope for a believer's life. To see only sin leads to masochism, and a consciousness of sin can assume sickly proportions. Even in this Psalm there's often success. I think of the joyous content of verses 9-10. But just as our Psalm ends with a question, so we often end with questions.

Indeed, not only this Psalm but the whole Bible closes with a question, not an answer. "Come, Lord Jesus!" What do we then hear? First of all, something very serious. We're reminded once more how much predestination means commission. Ultimately there's no place on earth for "dogs and sorcerers . . . and idolaters, and every one who loves and practices falsehood" (Rev. 22:15). Secondly, we hear something very joyous. After all the difficult things we've seen comes something very reassuring. We're graciously invited to "wash [our] robes"—*that opportunity exists* —"And let him who is thirsty come, let him who desires take the water of life without price" (Rev. 22:14, 17)! Predestination is indeed a commission and a task. We forget this too easily. But thereafter and therefore it's—and this first of all—a *gift*.

When we've realized all this it will make us so happy that we'll begin to cry, "Come, Lord Jesus! Come quickly! While in the roll of the book it is also written about me, it is written especially about You!"

WHO DOES GOOD MEETS GOOD

"Blessed is he who considers the poor!
The Lord delivers him in the day of trouble . . ."

—Psalm 41:1

Who does good meets good. Is that true? It's not the whole truth but it is a truth with which we have to reckon. It's certainly not nonsense, though we can often deal with it nonsensically (pharisaically, neo-colonially, racially, etc.). It's a truth that often comes to light. It's a truth by which we can make many friends. It's a truth by which parents can bind children to themselves— and not just a little. On the other hand, it's something about which children can have the greatest expectations. Anyone who does good by honoring his parents can count on a "long life." That evokes an enormous piece of existence.

Impressive examples

This last applied not only to the world of the Old Testament but holds true for what we call the new covenant, for it is still "the first commandment with promise" (Eph. 6:2), as Paul says. We can expect a lot from it not only in the narrower relationships of a family; it also holds true in larger relationships, for example, in politics. The same Paul says: "if your enemy is hungry, feed him . . . *for by so doing you will heap burning coals upon his head"* (Rom. 12:20). *Christian* politics is often also the best *politics!* Since we may be skeptical about applying this to politics, take another example—the church. The early Christian church attracted attention because it spent itself in doing good. That's how it came to be in "favor with all the people" and how "the Lord added to their number day by day those who were being saved" (Acts 2:47). It's hard to exaggerate the effect implied in the saying "Who does good meets good."

Ingratitude the way of the world

Yet it's not the whole truth. Unhappily, something else is also true. We can expect much but not everything by practicing the aforementioned proverb. In John 15:20 we hear Jesus say—and it's certainly meant as a prophecy of the times in which we still live—" 'A servant is not greater than his master.' If they persecuted me, they will persecute you." It's clear what kind of master is meant here—the *good* master, the *good* shepherd. It's also clear what kind of servants are meant—people enslaved to the goodness of that master! Finally, it's clear that this goodness can and indeed will evoke oppression in the world, and therefore will not always be understood but also hated and despised.

This applies not only to Christians when they try to do good. It applies to everyone who makes goodness his business. In the world goodness is not only the business of Christians. It's the business of Jesus Christ, the Lord. But He's not only the Lord of Christians. He gives out His good outside our circles just as there too He burdens people with the suffering that may be provoked by this (along with the blessing).

Accordingly, while we can often confess that "Who does good meets good," we'll also have to confess that "Ingratitude is the way of the world." The latter is the experience of our poet. He doesn't even talk about bitter experiences in general which he's had for practicing goodness. He talks—and that says a great deal—about what he discovered about his friends with whom he thought he had shared this good. It isn't very pleasant. "Even my bosom friend in whom I trusted, who ate of my bread, has lifted his heel against me." He says this while maintaining his own "integrity" three verses later on. This is already apparent from the

fact that the professed friend ate his (the poet's) bread. The poet
is a generous man who understands integrity not simply as "doing
no evil" but as "doing good," and for whom this is synonymous
with generosity and mercy.

Who does good meets God

One might suggest that the poet doesn't so much intend to say,
"Who does good meets good," as to say, "Who does good meets
God." It certainly would be easier to derive the latter from the
first three verses of the Psalm than the former. In any case, it is
safer, and let no one say this doesn't change things! Then the
promise that someone hangs over his head reads: "In his illness
thou changest all his bed" (R.S.V. margin). That's a great difference! It doesn't assume a believer's good makes him immune to
suffering and mishap, but it does mean that suffering and mishap
are seen in different light. He may count on the special care of
God in such suffering and mishap.

Who says all this?

However, even this truth doesn't seem to come easily for the
poet. He's not able to maintain even this conviction altogether.
After the healing language of the first three verses we hear him
complain in verse 4, "As for me, I said, 'O LORD, be gracious to
me; *heal me* . . .'" We also hear it honestly stated where this
complaint is stuck, "for I have sinned against thee!" And this
from a man who in verse 12 had appealed to his own integrity before God! He doesn't say, "Heal me, for I'm innocent." He says,
"Lord, heal me, for I have sinned!"

One need not exclude the other. Undoubtedly the poet is a man
who has done a great deal for his neighbor in the sphere of love.
But it didn't go to his head. He realizes that our achievements in
the sphere of goodness are and remain but patchwork. Who then
can say, "Who does good meets good"? Only someone who
doesn't always try to begin with the latter half of the saying, even
if we substitute "God" for "good," because he isn't always trying

to assume that he's the one described in the first half of the
saying.

Matthew 25

Thus our truism is and remains but a partial truth. Yet I'm not
saying this correctly. One day it will be the whole truth—so Jesus
tells us in Matthew 25:31-46, when He speaks of the judgment of
the Son of man.

He understands the fulfillment of our saying for He is the
source of another saying that is as like it as two peas in a pod.
"Blessed are the merciful, for they shall obtain mercy" (Matt.
5:7). What occurs then makes us think in striking manner of our
text. The verse: "Blessed is he who considers the poor! The LORD
delivers him in the day of trouble" is then clarified in a special
way. What is more "the day of trouble" than the day of the last
judgment? And when will the "blessed" be pronounced more
compellingly and blessedly than on that day?

In that "blessed" we should not think only of God and of the
good there is because it's *good to be near Him* (Ps. 73:28). Ultimately the meaning is not that one who does good only meets
God. He also meets "the" good—and a partial truth becomes the
whole truth. What the biblical word "blessed" includes is not only
a matter of God and heaven but also of earthly fulfillment. That's
what the poet is pointing toward, and we with him. Jesus too
wants us to see it this way, when He says to those at the close of
the age, "Come, O blessed of my Father, *inherit the kingdom prepared for you*" (Matt. 25:34). That's not only about God but
about His kingdom. That's already clear from another proclamation about blessedness our Savior addressed to the same people—
"Blessed are the meek, for *they shall inherit the earth.*"

One thing more

As we said earlier, what a change it makes if someone who
does good meets God even if he meets no other good, even if he's
spared neither suffering nor mishap. At least the poet found that

"his bed was changed"! However, the greatest change is reserved for those who, when Jesus says they paid attention to Him because they—like the poet—have paid attention to the poor, answer in astonishment that this relationship had quite escaped them (Matt. 25:37-38). That is to say, they had not realized He was behind it all. They had not realized that by doing good they had garnered so much good, so much blessedness, for themselves. Why call this a change? Because astonishment is the greatest change there is.

But didn't we hear in the Psalm that the perfect mercy cannot be reached here and that even people who walk in integrity—in greatest generosity—must still confess sin? That one doesn't exclude the other (cf. 1 John 1:8 and 2:9) could be the most astonishing feature of what will happen "When the Son of man comes in his glory" (Matt. 25:31)!

HOMESICKNESS AND HOPE

*"Why are you cast down, O my soul,
and why are you disquieted within me?
Hope in God . . ."*

—Psalm 42:5, 11; 43:5

The Psalmist feels lost, estranged from his origin, driven away. He's almost had it! That's the way he feels about himself. In Psalm 42:7, we hear that he's submerged by floods. In verse 9, that he goes about in mourning—and not because of others but because of himself. He feels estranged from everything and especially from Zion. He can't reach Zion anymore. He's far away in the land of Jordan and the mountains of Hermon. That's the region east of the Jordan, the northern part of that region, where the river has its source and where Caesarea Philippi was later built. He could not be farther from the centrum (Zion).

Then and now

However, that's not why he feels so estranged. It's because people say to him, not once but continually, "Where is your God?" That's what he calls the "deadly wound in my body." That's the real reason he goes about in mourning. A moment ago we said he felt estranged not because of others but because of himself. Actually, that's not quite true. He is in mourning for God. *God* has become rather dead for him. Not only for others—but for him. Their cry, "Where is God?" is taken over by him when we hear him say, "Why hast thou forgotten me?"

A great homesickness has taken hold of him. It's a homesickness for "then," when everything was different and better. Listen to him: "These things I remember, as I pour out my soul: how I went with the throng, and led them in procession to the house of God, with glad shouts and songs of thanksgiving, with a multitude keeping festival." If you please! We would say: once he went ahead with music but now he feels (vs. 7) like a drowned cat or, to stay with the more familiar and attractive image of Psalm 42, like a hart that pants (Dutch: cries) for flowing streams.

Indeed, where is God?

The question of our Psalm, "Where is God?"—posed by others but appropriated by the poet—is not unfamiliar for it stabs us too. We're acquainted with it. It may be circumstances that force the question upon us. The poet feels himself "far gone" not only because he's separated from Zion, but because he feels sick, even dying. That's what we could conclude from Psalm 42:7. All sorts of circumstances are against him. It might also be people who force the question upon you. The "deceitful and unjust men" play their part in Psalms 42 and 43 (which we take together because originally they were a single Psalm).

All sorts of events and encounters bring the question to our lips: what has become of God in all of these events and encounters? A man then feels "far gone." He can also get the impression that "then" everything was different and better, and that faith has lessened rather than increased with the years. Once faith was young and fresh; now it's old and faded, if not actually dying. We can apply all this to ourselves, to the whole church, asking ourselves if "then" everything wasn't very different and better. Then church going was more like verse 4, like a musical corps. Now it's more like a few drops dripping from a faucet—a few folks still go to church on Sunday but soon even that will be over. Indeed, what has become of God?

Comfort

And yet, there's also comfort here. To begin, there's the famil-

iar comfort of which we've spoken before, meager but not insignificant. A question like "What has become of God?", brought about
by a forsaken feeling that we're "far gone" for whatever reason, is
not just a modern question. We thought it was. We thought we
had discovered the absence of God in the 1950's and 1960's. Apparently the question is ages old, as is the homesickness connected
with it. That's a bit comforting. Accordingly, we may not say that
everything is going downhill, that soon nothing will be left of
faith and church. Some three thousand years ago people already
thought so. No, such temptations are not limited to recent times,
even if we've thought so in an a-historical manner that has much
in common with pride as well—if that's not the same thing—as
with self-torment.

Still, this is but meager comfort if it doesn't include something
more. And it does. After all, if this temptation can't be called typically modern, then this faith can't be called typically old-fash-
ioned—something my grandfather understood, my father a bit
less, and I no longer at all. Let's have an even exchange! If today's temptations are already present in the Psalms, then the faith
of the Psalms is also contemporary. That's why we may not only
conclude: then everything was as bad as today—that would be
poor comfort indeed—we must also say now too there's every reason to believe, just as then. Faith? Yes. Because hope, and in the
Bible hope is the same as faith.

Listen!

The same poet who says in Psalm 42:3 that he can cry day
and night says, in verse 8, that it's not his tears which have been
his meat day and night but rather God's steadfast love. That is to
say, He smiles through his tears! God has remained good to him,
and his loving-kindness is first of all evident in the fact that he
can still pray. That doesn't mean he's any less chock-full of questions but it does mean that he has an address for his questions—a
rock of an address! The consequences of this are considerable.

Three times we hear the familiar: "Why are you cast down, O

my soul, and why are you disquieted within me? Hope in God; for I shall again praise him, my help and my God." The question is a rhetorical question, meaning: "Don't carry on this way, O my soul!—how would God ever have forsaken you?" That's the first thing to be said. In the second place, a climax appears in the question. First we hear something negative: "Why are you cast down, O my soul, and why are you disquieted within me?" Then follows something positive: "Hope in God," and then comes the climax: "for I shall again praise him, my help and my God." The question smells of the answer!

This climax—and that's the third thing—doesn't only come from *within* the question, it also comes in between those questions that are repeated three times in Psalms 42 and 43. The first two times the question is submerged under the fact that the poet's soul is bowed down again (42:6; 43:1). The last time, however, it remains standing upright with all the answers included in it. The soul scolded in faith is not brought to its knees again. One day we'll remain standing!

Hope and homesickness

How does the poet come to this faith and to this hope? Through his homesickness, I think. He must have been overcome by thoughts like this: "That faith and that church—that was really something!" Naturally, we have to appreciate the consuming homesickness of this man! He's literally wasting away in his thirst for God. He can't "eat for his tears" any longer. It's all too much for him. And you know: he who seeks finds in the gospel, and he who asks receives answer.

Is that also true for the question "Where is God?" Is it true for the question about "the absence of God"? Yes, for this question also, for where is God *not* present? Jesus said something like that —and He ought to know. Was He not at home with God? He had something to say to someone who was also a stranger and who also thought the God of Israel could only be found in Jerusalem, in Zion—I'm thinking of the Samaritan woman—whereas the God of Israel is nowhere more *present* than at the cross *outside* Jerusalem! And what did Jesus give to this strange "hind" who was thirsting? The water of life freely (John 4:10)!

Robust praise

How do these Psalms end? Where do they lead? To praise—praise with a cither! We meet such praise with cither somewhere else, in the Book of Revelation (15:2). It's a very robust praise, for it's like "the voice of a great multitude, like the sound of many waters and like the sound of mighty thunderpeals" (Rev. 19:6).

That is to say, this praise knows what to do with the multitude that asks, "Where is God," just as it knows what to do with the voice of the many waters of death in Psalm 42:7, and as it knows what to do with all sorts of thunderous things that come upon us. This praise is so robust that it overpowers everything. Although this is a vision of the future it can already be heard by those who are wasted not only by homesickness but also with longing. And the former doesn't exclude the latter, but includes it.

STRANGE GODS

*"If we had forgotten the name of our God,
or spread forth our hands to a strange god,
would not God discover this?"*

—Psalm 44:20-21

Speaking of other, strange gods—did Israel think that they existed? It's a well-known question when dealing with the first commandment—whether we should take this commandment monotheistically or monolatristically. Did Israel believe there was actually one God, or did Israel believe that perhaps there were many gods but that it served only One? To tell the truth, we can't be sure. Stories like that of the covenant between Jacob and Laban, described as between "The God of Abraham and the God of Nahor" (Gen. 31:53) do not allow us to simply dismiss the second view (namely, that perhaps we should read the first commandment in terms of monolatry). In that event, the point of the story would be that Jacob swears by "the Fear of his father Isaac." That's enough for him, even though there be a thousand gods of Nahor!

No other gods any longer?

The question is not out of date because the various gods do not seem to be out of date. After Paul wrote (in terms of monotheism) to Corinth: "we know that 'an idol has no real existence,' and that 'there is no God but one,' " he added (in terms of monolatry), "For although there may be many so-called gods in heaven and on earth—as indeed there are many 'gods' and many 'lords' —yet for us there is one God, the Father . . ." (1 Cor. 8:4-6).

I would not dare say we no longer have other gods or that Christ's fear of mammon (Matt. 6:24), for example, is out of date. Doesn't Donar sometimes haunt us, or Mars, or Eros? Are we rid of the fear of the elemental spirits, of lust and strife, of consuming passions? Don't we too have to say that in actuality there are more than One, even if ultimately we serve but One? That is, *if* we can still say this! Doesn't it seem sometimes more serious—namely, that although there may be only the One, in actuality there are many whom we serve?

Two masters

The poet says, I and my people spread forth our hands to the One.

He adds something to this—namely, that anything else is really impossible because God will always discover it.

That's how we have to look at it. God will always discover it even if I have not. The latter is often the case. When we commit idolatry, we never do this so blatantly as "to imagine something in which to put our trust" *in place of* the one true God, as the Heidelberg Catechism says on Sunday 34. But we often put this *beside* Him, as the Catechism adds realistically.

God would then be pushed into the position of a rival by our loves, not by the way we associate with these in themselves (since as such they're usually granted us), but by the way in which we're stuck to them and enslaved by them, letting everything stand or fall with them (our humor, happiness, security), by the *religious* attachment they (our marriage, position, Nato, corpus christianum) can receive. Ultimately, to put "beside Him" is the same as to put "in place of Him," since ultimately "No one can serve two masters; for either he will hate the one and love the other, or he will be devoted to the one and despise the other. You cannot serve God and mammon," as Jesus said (Matt. 6:24).

The strange God

But suppose the opposite happens. Suppose our problem is not

that we let ourselves be taken in by strange gods—to act as if
these exist and are still active—but that God Himself, the only
true God, should become strange to us, looking so terribly different that we no longer can follow Him? Suppose that we're in danger of losing our faith in Him and that He is in danger of becoming
a no-God to us? Something like this must have vexed the poet
when, after his exclamation, we hear him complain, "Rouse thyself! Why sleepest thou, O Lord?"

That sounds familiar. Who else could complain that their God
was asleep? When discussing Psalm 28, we reminded ourselves
that the priests of Baal did this. We hear something of our poet's
words in their cry, "Baal, answer us! (1 Kings 18:26). Then it
was the prophet who suggested mockingly that maybe their god
was asleep. There's a lot in that. It's characteristic of false gods to
be asleep and not to be "with it," and it's characteristic of the
God of Israel that he will "neither slumber nor sleep" (Ps. 121:4)!
But what about the sleeping God in our Psalm? Has our God become like Baal and become strange to us? If so, our faith too
would be superstition!

In the storm

Who else thought their God was asleep? Not only the poet, but
also disciples in the storm (Mark 4:35-41). They were as nervous about their Lord and Master as were the priests of Baal about
their god.

We must begin by recognizing that it was true. Jesus was
asleep. Can we simply say this about God? No, we cannot. Perhaps we can say something else. Perhaps God sometimes wants us
to think so. Why? So that we become rattled? I don't think so.
Quite the contrary! So that we may be prodded to greater activity.
Various references in the Bible suggest that God draws back, as it
were, not to goad us to despairing passivity but rather to goad us
to a faithful "I'll take my stand!" For example, we hear something
like this in our Lord's farewell, in which He says that it is to our
"advantage" that He leave (John 16:7). He prepares the way for
the activity of the Holy Spirit—the verse makes clear that there is

a causal relationship—and what else is this if not the *Acts* of the Apostles? *God Has Gone Abroad* is the title of a brochure by a minister to students, Dr. A. W. Cramer, who links the title to various parables of Jesus. This "going abroad" of the Lord is not a provocation to defeat, unbelief, or despair. It's rather a summons directed to servants to be active, an acknowledgment that *our* activity is generously granted and desired by God. Little wonder that the storm at sea ends with a rebuke to disciples. *Not* that the storm was a punishment for their sin—that's no more the case there than the oppression of people in our Psalm. The poet experienced this almost as though it were a natural disaster like a storm. In the gospel story, we have to think not about our own guilt, nor directly about God's will, but about the activity of the devil. The disciples are put in their place not because of a link between the storm and their unbelief, but because of a link between always calling on God and unbelief—unbelief in the sense that they refused to trust the portion of endurance and maturity granted to and demanded of us by God. Might Calvin, who—as we saw in Psalm 39—sometimes complains about the Psalmist's unbelief, be right this time?

In Gethsemane

The story of the storm at sea is of interest in relation to our text. Of more interest in this connection, however, is the story of Gethsemane. That story tells us what happens when it really matters, when the greatest storm arises and the greatest oppression. Notice. Then it's we who are asleep while the Lord is awake! He would have appreciated it had we been able to watch with Him "one hour" (Matt. 26:40). But we couldn't even manage that. When it really matters, it's not we who are the slaughtered sheep (Ps. 44:22; Rom. 8:36), but *He* (Isa. 53; John 1:29). Often God's "sleeping" is related to our "watching" as watching to sleeping! When it really matters, we behave more strangely than God. When all is said and done, who gives us so much reason to trust him as the God and Father of Jesus Christ? No other god can ever get hold of us again. We'd better watch out!

A WEDDING SONG

". . . forget your people and your father's house;
and the king will desire your beauty.
Since he is your lord . . ."

—Psalm 45:10-11

What excites our attention at a wedding? Why do even outsiders hope to catch a glimpse at the steps of the court house or at the church door? That's not hard to answer. What excites attention at a wedding is the beauty of the bride. The interesting thing is not that we think this important but that apparently the Bible isn't embarrassed to call attention to it and make a great deal of it. Apparently the Bible isn't content only to dote upon inward beauty. Calvin must have been more "biblical" than the Bible when, while looking and letting others help him look for a wife, he was only interested in the spiritual and useful qualities of one with whom to share his life. A beautiful girl is something to see, the Bible says (Song of Sol. 6:13). Beauty is something to brag about. It's no accident that we hear the daughters of Job were the fairest in the land (Job 42:15). That sounds a bit like a fairy tale. They must have been as beautiful as fairy queens! And we're not even sure that all this was simply natural! What someone doesn't have naturally may be beautified in all sorts of ways. This is evident when we hear the name of one of Job's daughters is Kerenhappuch (eye shadow), a name that smells of a whole cosmetics table (Job 42:14)!

A knight without fear or fault

This quality is appreciated not only in brides but also in the bridegroom. In our Psalm not only the bride but also the bridegroom is praised for his beauty (vss. 2, 8, etc.).

We may feel that beauty isn't enough, and we've always felt this about even the loveliest stories. What do we look for in a knight? Not only outward appearance—his height, with which he can both charm and win in tournament. We think not only of that *by* which he can win all to him, but also *for what,* the *cause* for which he stands. A knight is only a true knight if he's a "knight without fear or fault." This is certainly desirable if the knight is more than a knight and if—as in the case of our Psalm—he's a king. That's why we not only hear talk about his outward luster but also about that for which he does battle, the splendid cause of "truth, meekness, and justice." We hear that he's someone who not only loves the beauty of his bride but who also loves "righteousness" and hates "wickedness."

Where have we heard this?

Not only of the bridegroom is more required than a striking appearance. The same is true of the bride. We hear this in the verse we've chosen as our theme, verse 10: "forget your people and your father's house."

These are familiar words which we recall from somewhere and which make us think of something else. In the Bible a bride represents something more. After all the very earthy comments we've made, we may now point to something beyond this. In the Bible the bride represents the people of God, the church, of whom it's written that she is so beautiful that she's "in splendor, without spot or wrinkle or any such thing" (Eph. 5:27). Just read Psalms 48 and 87! Similarly, in the Bible the bridegroom represents no one less than God Himself, the knight par excellence, "without fear or fault."

All this brings us back to Genesis 12:1 where we read: "Now

the LORD said to Abram, 'Go from your country and your kindred and your father's house to the land that I will show you.' " The nuptial proposal made in our Psalm, with all it includes, reminds us of the nuptial proposal Abraham received, and Abraham is the father of the faithful. But we're not only led back into the Old Testament. We're led forward into the New Testament, where we hear Jesus say: "He who loves father or mother more than me is not worthy of me" (Matt. 10:37).

Pure relativists

We must pause here. How are we to interpret this? It's possible to interpret and experience this in rather bitter manner. The distance to which the bride of Christ, the church, is called with regard to concerns of blood and soil can turn out to be very difficult if she's to follow her Lord unconditionally and be desirable in His eyes. Yes, it's possible—not only for God to be desirable in our eyes, but for us to be desirable in His! But we recognize how hard this distance can be in the words Jesus utters immediately prior to Matthew 10:37. He says: "For I have come to set a man against his father, and a daughter against her mother, and a daughter-in-law against her mother-in-law; and a man's foes will be those of his own household." We can imagine what our Bridegroom's cause— the cause of "truth, meekness, and justice"—cost whole families during the 1930's and 1940's. The two-edged sword of our Hero was drawn through all of it. For that matter, think what his departure cost Abraham!

We don't have to experience all of this so bitterly. We don't have to leave the concerns of blood and soil literally and physically to know that a reserve is commanded and that this is what's at stake here. This king demands everything, even the shirt off our back—with the result that everything else is no longer "everything." This king makes his appearance so absolutely in our life that by comparison all else must become relative. In this sense one can argue that believers are the most complete and pure relativists there are.

In the light of this marriage, it also holds true for our own marriage. In Christian marriage a husband cannot mean everything to his wife, or vice versa; while Christ may not say this in so many words, it's certainly implied. If anyone still doubts this, he should read Paul's letter to the Corinthians, where we hear him say: "let those who have wives live as though they had none." We'll enjoy even our marriage with a certain reserve. It must not become everything to us. And where else does this reserve *not* apply? Paul continues: "and those who mourn as though they were not mourning, and those who rejoice as though they were not rejoicing, and those who buy as though they had no goods, and those who deal with the world as though they had no dealings with it" (1 Cor. 7:29-31).

While this need not mean the bitterness of a literal separation or the withholding of love, sexuality, and all that makes life ferment and cook and bubble—even though one can picture situations where this becomes literally necessary—in any case it means that we may take life seriously, with all its joys and all its sorrows, but not "dead serious" (i.e., ultimately so). We may not *believe* in our marriage, our joy, our sorrow, our job—no matter how ideal—in the same way we believe in Him with whom everything ultimately stands or falls.

More sweet than sour

If not bitter, this may sound a bit sour. Yet it's more sweet than sour. Whoever reaches a hand to Him, whoever surrenders all his loves to this great Lover, receives everything back de-divinized and de-demonized (and that's the same thing). We receive it back made to measure so that we know how to handle it, so we don't expect too much of it or limit ourselves to it, so that we can *meet* everything with a glorious relativism. That also means we can meet it with a great deal of humor, which is the best distance there is. We know it's not our relativism which is the guarantee of God's absoluteness. What a poor idea that would be of Him! Rather, His absoluteness is the guarantee of our blessed and pure human relativism! The fact that a husband and wife have learned from Him (of whom they cannot ask too much) not to ask too much of each other enables them to travel together toward a happy marriage.

Liberated by the great redeemer of all that cramps our life, we can now travel toward sorrow and joy to the world of commerce and art and ideals. Not romantically or cynically, but soberly. And now we'll be able to take it! Nor will we get away from the song, as perhaps we had feared, but we'll come to it now in marvelous manner as we seem to have come to a wedding feast whose joy exceeds that of Psalm 45 by far.

THE FIERCE GOD

"Come, behold the works of the Lord,
how he has wrought desolations in the earth."

—Psalm 46:8

The verse we have chosen for discussion has a fierce sound. What are we to make of it? Do desolations on earth come from God? Must we think of Him as the final cause behind every ruin? Were the folks in Tholen right in appealing to the Heidelberg Catechism (Sunday 10), where I read that all sorts of desolations like "drought, unfruitful years, sickness, and poverty" come to us from God? And not from some arbitrary God but—and that's the problem—from a fatherly God, as we read in Answer 27 of the Catechism? Were those parents in Tholen right when they even thought the polio with which their children were visited came from God while vaccinations came from false gods? Or haven't we read the text correctly?

Not read correctly

Indeed, we have not read it correctly. We've not only read it incorrectly but have even read the opposite of what's there!

That is to say, it's not enough to say that, though desolations on earth come from God, the opposite is happily also true according to the following verse 9. There we read that God, who brings desolations according to verse 8, is the same God who makes wars to cease to the end of the earth. God would then be the builder as well as the wrecker. I find that poor comfort, more tragic than saving.

No. Happily that's not what it says either. That wouldn't bring us to the opposite of where we began. At most we would have a supplement, albeit a happy supplement—but only a supplement that would not negate what was posited earlier—namely, that desolation comes on earth because of God. Verses 8 and 9 would then have approximately equal weight.

Happily that's not the way it is. The truth of verse 8 is meaningless without that of verse 9. The accent doesn't lie on bringing desolations but wholly on making them cease! We can say confidently that verse 8 is wholly taken up in verse 9, is wholly in its service. J. Ridderbos is entirely correct when he puts verses 8-11 in his commentary under the heading "Yahweh, king of the realm of peace." Notice—verses 8-11, not 9-11!

Judgment

However, if God is to establish this realm of peace and an eventual end of desolations, He must first, no matter how much He hates it, smash a great deal that has to be cleared away. It's not evil as such that comes to us from God's hand but judgment in particular does—and that's not the same thing! It follows that God doesn't bring desolations on earth because they're His good pleasure and as though we must on that account just let them be. If He is fierce, it's for a different reason—not on His own initiative but in reaction, because the earth and its people *ask* for it!

Someone may ask whether there are not untold instances in the Bible that point to a very close relation between God and evil, even a direct primary relation. Amos 3:6 is often cited: "Does evil befall a city, unless the LORD has done it?" If we don't take this verse out of context we'll notice that the context is again one of judgment.

Speaking of desolations, however, doesn't that sound very primary, coming directly from God, as in Genesis 1:2: "The earth was without form and void"? Didn't God make the creation itself a wild and fierce creation? No, that's not what it says. We can read it along these lines: something—desolation and void—threatens us in creation as a judgment *apart from* God the Creator. Without Him we would all become nihilists—falling into ruin, even into dust.

The Catechism about evil

In this connection, Sunday 10, as also Sunday 9 of the Heidelberg Catechism, can lead to misunderstanding by stating that evil comes to us by God's direction. I don't believe this can or should be said so simply and baldly. Fortunately! I think the folks in Tholen forgot this. They attributed everything to God so quickly that they forgot man's share in it.

Let's not make it more difficult than it is. To whom must we look for the cause when children get polio if not to those who neglected vaccination, no matter how cruel and sad this may sound? We have to look to them in general and to their leaders in particular.

To do otherwise not only would forget man's share in the evil that occurs on earth, but also would forget the devil's share. Significantly, even the Heidelberg Catechism—which elsewhere remembers this—seems to have forgotten it when portraying God's part in evil on Sundays 9 and 10. Yet the devil plays an enormous role in it—witness that section of the Bible in which evil also plays an enormous role, the Book of Job. The language of Sunday 1 of the Catechism is more careful than that of Sundays 9 and 10. There I read that "without the will of my Father in heaven not a hair can fall from my head," and that sounds very different. It doesn't mean that when a hair falls from my head it happens *by* God's will. That not one sparrow falls to the ground "without your Father's will" (Matt. 10:29) need not mean *God* lets sparrows fall to the ground. It does mean that, when sparrows fall to the ground, *God can still will to do something with what happens.*

Against, not outside

For Bavinck, evil was something that has a place *against* God's will, but is not *outside* His will. Along this line we may seek a solution for that strange word in Isaiah (45:7) which says that God "creates" evil. Given the fact that everywhere else in Scripture God battles evil and expressly commands men "to purge the evil from Israel" (Deut. 22:22), this can only mean He can take care of it and, more than that, can also make something of it! The church's suffering, of which Peter writes, is in itself a temptation (1 Peter 1:6). As such it comes from the devil, for God tempts no one (James 1:13). But God is "man enough" to will something with it—namely, that in this suffering one should follow in the footsteps of Christ (1 Peter 3:17; 4:19). No one would ever get it into his head to suggest that in some way God willed the gassing of seven million Jews. Nevertheless, even with this utterly devilish thing, He has been able to do something with it—the establishment of the state of Israel, and the desert to begin blossoming like a rose!

Jesus about evil

We must also observe the way in which Jesus hated suffering and was taken aback by it (John 11:33-36). He even hated evil in the form of judgment, as instruction, for our good. Before He prophesied Jerusalem's destruction (Matt. 24:2), He still sought to woo her to Himself with the words: "O Jerusalem, Jerusalem, killing the prophets and stoning those who are sent to you! How often would I have gathered your children together as a hen gathers her brood under her wings, and you would not" (Matt. 23:37)!

Someone will ask whether sickness and such desolation are not part of God's creation. We said that polio came to Tholen thanks to the parents—but they didn't invent the bacillus! That's true. Still, we've never really been satisfied with the idea that sickness is part of the creation. In the long run, we should not trust biologists any more than theologians! We've always sensed something devil-

ish in sickness and in the dreadful way in which a man can become acquainted with it. And we're not alone in this. Jesus sees a
strong bond between disease and devil.

But, assuming we can understand a judgment in sickness—not
personally but in general—has God willed that? I would not want
to think of judgment immediately when thinking of the devil,
though I do believe that God can box our ears with devilish judgments. But His heart isn't in it, for with one hand He gives the
pain and with the other the medicine. Apparently He's stuck with it.

1939-1945

We close with an example quite in keeping with our Psalm,
since the latter is a war song. Did God will that war should break
out in 1939? We'd rather say, No, the Germans willed that. Did
the allies will that the war should end in 1945? Yes, but we'd
rather say God willed this. To whose account shall we reckon the
desolations of 1939-1945 in Europe and beyond? We would say
the Germans were responsible. With one exception—their own
desolations came to them on God's account, from the fierce God
who wanted peace so fiercely in Europe and beyond. We could
sing Luther's hymn at the liberation, "A Mighty Fortress Is Our
God." We had more reason to do so than Luther, for the Anti-
christ he thought opposed him pales into a saint compared with
the devil who entered into Adolf Hitler. That's how simply and
severely the God of the Psalms wants us to see things.

Not done with it

Even so, we're not yet done with it. Judgment and desolation
not only touch others—they touch me. Jesus' word, "I have not
come to bring peace, but a sword" (Matt. 10:34) touches me
first of all! One does the Germans no favor by being pro-German,
and one does himself no favor by not being anti-oneself. What all
will I not have to experience before there is peace? I have to experience my own death. One day someone will stand by my ruins.

Fierce and fast

Fortunately, the Lord our God is a God who knows when to stop! Our Psalm deals not only with the past but with the future. It can't be pinned down to a single datum. It doesn't want to be read simply historically, for it bursts through the seams of history. It's simply not placeable—it's eschatological. There is a remainder. One day the sea in verse 3 which makes even the mountains quake (image of demonic power) will be silent. Revelation 21:1 tells us that "the sea was no more." In verse 4 of our Psalm the image of the raging sea abruptly gives way to the more peaceful image of a river, the image of a peace that passes understanding (Phil. 4:7), the image of "the water of life" (Rev. 22:1). Yes, the Lord our God knows when to stop. The image of the one will be changed into the image of the other—more abruptly than in our Psalm—"in a moment" of time (1 Cor. 15:52). One day there will be peace.

If God would work fiercely in my life again—and if I'm sure it's God who is fierce (because that's not always obvious)—then I have to remember that He is busy with *that* goal and is intent on that. Then something festive becomes part of the desolation, a bit of Advent. For who or what is this fierce God if not a swift God? Who or what is this fierce God if not He of whom it is written, "Surely I am coming soon" (Rev. 22:20)!

THE CHURCH AND POLITICS

"Clap your hands, all peoples!"

—Psalm 47:1

This Psalm is a strange whole. First we hear that all peoples are invited to clap their hands. Then we hear that these same peoples must bow under the yoke of Israel, not only bow but be trodden under foot. Finally we hear that genuine existence and autonomy are not granted them any longer for the princes of the peoples are gathered "as the people of the God of Abraham." Doubtless the mention of the ascent of God is linked with this. This would point to the joyous procession of the ark, the symbolic witness to God's presence, to Zion after the enemy has been defeated.

Context

What is the context? J. Ridderbos sees so little relation to context that in verses 1 and 9 he takes "peoples" to refer to the tribes of Israel, while verse 3 refers to other "peoples." Otherwise one would wonder why they are to clap their hands. In view of all that occurs, we can imagine people answering, "Never!" To be quite honest, that's the way we Christians approach people around us, people we assume will react to the gospel message with a "Never!" We're not even surprised by that any longer. We think we understand it completely even if, little by little, understanding becomes approving.

The courage of redemption

Perhaps a better solution is possible. The poet, with the best will in the world, can't imagine what we think we can imagine. With the best will in the world, he simply can't imagine that the peoples of the world ultimately won't let themselves be won over to the God of Israel. We could say that Bavinck's joyous word, "No one may believe he is rejected," applies also to unbelievers. That has something to say to missions and evangelism. We dare not go as far toward universalism as Barth, but we can learn from him, for in his joyous fight against unbelief he comes close to our poet. Israel knew occasions when her expectations of faith about the unbelief of the nations could be compared with those of Monica regarding her unbelieving son, Augustine. That mother of Augustine must have been a courageous woman for it wasn't a promising outlook when she began. It was just as courageous for Israel, that little cockleshell in a sea of nations, for the outlook wasn't promising. Courage and humor—that's what faith is like. It has the courage of redemption.

Therefore, Ridderbos notwithstanding, we'll assume there is a connection between the clapping of hands and the putting under foot, just as there is a connection between the putting under foot and what follows. As we see it, it's not a gloomy but a glorious thing to be lifted up as the people of Abraham. The connection is so close that we dare believe it refers to one and the same people, the people of mankind.

The connection is that of losing life and finding it (Matt. 10:34), a connection for which we don't need to wait till we come to the New Testament. The prophet Joel also calls our attention to it when he first (2:12-17) brings us under the claim of repentance—a claim that must rend hearts as well as garments, from which even children are not exempt, and so urgent that bride and bridegroom are not even granted a wedding night—such is the final gravity of the claim.

But then we meet the prophet's dream of a worldwide festival that we have called Pentecost (Joel 2:28-32). The one is tied to the other. It becomes clear, as in the Psalm, that if there is men-

tion of formidable humiliation, there is also mention of limitless
exaltation. If in verse 4 only Jacob is called the pride of Jacob, in
verse 9 everyone is called this! Now there's no mention of humiliation but only of redemption. Pointing to Psalm 99:1, J. Ridderbos says: "By throne we must think first of all of the mercy seat
with the cherubim, which is often called the throne of God."
When it comes to redemption it's odd that this writer, who in
Psalm 1 pointed us so explicitly to the Epistle of John, does not
think here of 1 John 2:2: "and he is the expiation for our sins,
and not for ours only, but for the sins of the whole world." Instead, he carries forward his question, "How can the princes of
the peoples be called the people of Abraham? The latter must be
Israel!" This leads him to the conclusion that we're dealing here
with the tribes of Israel and not with the peoples of the world.
For Luther there was no question but that it was the peoples of
the world who clap their hands in this Psalm: "It is also for their
benefit; for their sake also He will be exalted among the nations!"

Outside the church no salvation

Does this losing of life recommended for the peoples mean that
they must lose their own life in Israel and in the church if they
are to find life? Not exactly. *He* brings peoples under us, as we
read in verse 3, and *He* chooses an inheritance for us, as we read
in verse 4. The clapping of hands, the applause of the nations, is
for God. *He* is the one who is carried on the shoulders, so to
speak, in verse 5. This song of praise is not directly a Psalm of
praise to Israel but to the *God* of Israel.

And yet, we cannot separate the two entirely—on either side.
Ultimately the faithful are fellow laborers with their God (1 Cor.
3:9). Those who first allowed themselves to be led to the God of
Israel become His heralds who can be looked up to with some
envy. After all, it's about the God of *Israel* and about the gospel
of the church. The latter is also true. We don't come to God by
ourselves. Ultimately, "salvation is from the Jews" (John 4:22)
and outside the church—that is to say, apart from the church—

there is no salvation. I would never have come to faith, said
Augustine, if the church had not brought me into it. He must have
been thinking of his mother and not only of his mother Monica.
The Psalm not only praises God but celebrates the relation between God and His people no less than it celebrates the relation
between God and the nations. No wonder that it has found such a
large place in the liturgy of church and synagogue!

The church and politics

Finally, it becomes clear that we must not only think of souls
but of nations from the point of view of the church. Evangelism
and politics are not an either/or. Professor Van Ruler says that
the concern of the Psalms is for the heart while in the prophets it
is for the kingdom. Undoubtedly that's true, but in this Psalm the
concern is for the remotest reaches and for the conversion not
only of souls but of entire peoples. "Rulers also must be brought
to Christ," observes Luther, when speaking of this Psalm.

The church has its own views about politics. It thinks more
severely and gently about politics than politics itself. Both the terrible and the tender sides of the church's contribution to politics can
be found in this Psalm. Professor Hendrikus Berkhof was the subject of much discussion in his own church because he suggested
that anyone who did not agree with the Pastoral Letter of the
Synod of the Netherlands Reformed Church about nuclear armaments, forbidding the use of atomic weapons, really ought to sub-
mit a complaint and be carried as a "conscientious objector." Even
if one doesn't share the professor's enthusiasm for this document
one cannot evade the question of how far the church of today still
believes its own ethic about the nations. Perhaps the lack of belief
in this, along with a one-sided narrowing of salvation to missions
and evangelism, is one of the reasons why the church wins so little applause from the nations—and, what is worse—so little applause for God! When do we sing this Psalm? Often at the festival
of the ascension of our Lord who, on that occasion, said "All
power is given unto me in heaven and in earth" (Matt. 28:18,

K.J.V.). By this power we think first of all of the power of reconciliation, but we must also think of a *politics* of reconciliation.

As in our Psalm, this will be both hard and gentle for people
and for nations. One doesn't exclude the other. That doesn't matter, just so long as the joyful meaning of it all is clear. What the
church has to say and contribute "for the good of the peoples" in
politics is not insignificant. After all, how does Jesus become
Lord? Luther says: "By joyful singing and psalms, that is, by the
joyful preaching of the gospel."

That's what it says—so joyful it's almost frightening. It's as
though Christ *cannot* be Lord without the joyful contribution of
the church on all fronts. Just imagine!

THE CHURCH AND PRIDE

"Walk about Zion, go round about her . . ."

—Psalm 48:12

There is a great deal of criticism of the church today, perhaps even more by church people than by those outside the church. It's no exaggeration to say that criticism of the church has become a modern symptom. It may also be a symptom of weariness. What both have in common is that neither is very fruitful. In this they differ from legitimate and true criticism. There's only one thing worse today than this kind of criticism and that is, no criticism at all. There are people whom you'll never hear utter one bad word about the church, but you should see what they do and fail to do and leave undone. They're so lazy and so stupid that they're even too lazy and stupid to criticize their own laziness. That's why the criticism described above, no matter how poor and fashionable it may be, is quite understandable. It could be a reaction against a chauvinism that afflicted the churches before the war, over against the world and one another. The pity is that what is understandable is not necessarily good. We must not suppose that what was spoiled through the church's self-conceit before the war can be remedied now by abject humiliation. At least the pre-war arrogance had something high-spirited about it, compared with the post-war confession of guilt—especially when the latter is so easy. How can a genuine confession of guilt be easy? It often looks more like a bit of sickly self-flagellation. We could wish the church formerly had been less sure of itself and today a bit more sure.

Proud of the church

There's another reason why criticism that simply takes the form of throwing dirt on the church and fouling the nest isn't good. The Bible, aside from the needed criticism—which must be present because there's no love where there's no criticism—knows something else when it comes to the church, and that's a needed *pride*. We see that here. Our text is an introduction and invitation to come and see all sorts of things worth seeing in the church. Listen: "number her towers, consider well her ramparts, go through her citadels; that you may tell the next generation." First we must go back to the invitation itself to hear that we must "go round about" her. That's the place to begin.

Around it

There's something rewarding about this summons to "go round about her" which makes mockery of love of easy and hasty surrender. We cannot simply take a snapshot of the church. We cannot simply take passing notice of it. That's not only true of someone outside the church who thinks he can make a quick judgment about the church. It's just as true—perhaps more so—for those who have been in the church all their lives but for whom it's been no more than a snapshot, a hasty acquaintance, wasted years. The summons to "go round about" is an incentive to give oneself to a full commitment—not just on Sunday but all through the week, not simply by studying but by practicing or, if the shoe fits the other way, not simply by practicing but also by studying.

This does not exclude all that makes the church festive but rather includes it. The going around commanded here is *commanded,* not a bit of advice. There's too much at stake. What is commanded is a liturgical going around it and the liturgy is festive.

This doesn't mean it may not be painful. We have to move forward, else we'll not make it. To turn back halfway is impossible. We can't go back to our first profession of faith. We must not ask what all this may cost in time, money, energy, imagination, and humor—and still not ever be through with it or fully around her. That's why criticism of the church can never be absolute. You simply don't know what you're talking about! This holds true for your own church, let alone the universal church. It's simply impossible to see it all. At best this is only possible "with all the saints." With all Christians we can begin to appreciate "what is the breadth and length and height and depth." Of what? Of criticism? Not quite. Of love, Paul says (Eph. 3:18).

Counting towers

Towers are splendid things that catch our attention from a distance and provide a silhouette. Whoever takes the trouble, and here we take a plunge into church history—that's part of going around—to jot down some of the many outstanding things that have emerged in the church—count your blessings!—discovers that they can't be numbered.

In passing, we mention a few examples of what can happen when the church appeared on the landscape and influenced the silhouette of culture. When Constantine became the first Christian emperor in 312, there was a sudden end of something that had been considered normal for many years—the practice of throwing unwanted children on the dung hill. When the church penetrated the stone age culture of Bali, the realization suddenly dawned that a wife is worth more than a pig, and that two wives are less than one. Simon Vestdijk has written a volume that assumes the eventual disappearance of church and Christendom but which nonetheless has to admit that without church and Christendom we would still be "walking around in animal skins, believing in Woden and gambling away our wives and children." No, he adds, that wouldn't quite be the case. "We would long since have exterminated each other." Even those who, for one reason or other, have given up the faith are still compelled by the church—in their ethics, for example, and even in their protest—to live by it.

These are all towers that can be counted. They are much more important than the fact that a church can still erect a stone tower today. Could it be that all these stone projections distracted attention through the years too much from what actually can be seen by friend and foe alike? We know that of the towers described in our Psalm "there will not be left here one stone upon another" (Matt. 24:2). We know too that all this could happen and that still this Psalm and all it includes has outlived itself—indeed, has outlived *God's judgments* even to this day.

A view

The Psalm continues, "consider well her ramparts." They're still there! We would not have thought so, but the church is still there and it still has a view. In spite of assaults outside the gates (materialism, communism, humanism, atheism), and in spite of assaults within (spiritualism, capitalism, docetism), the church is still there. I know no view more trustworthy that smiles at me, that listens so carefully and looks so patiently, than the view of the communion of saints.

Riches

Are the barns we often despise actually palaces? Yes, for palaces presuppose riches—and riches are there, riches of faith, hope, and love. Just ask a pastor or an elder or a deacon or anyone who rejoices with those who rejoice and suffers with those who suffer (Rom. 12:15)—or become one yourself—and your head will swim with the riches of hearts and families. That was one reason why the church could become so vehement about the appearance of a faith healer like Thomas Osborn. Quite apart from jealousy, it reacted to the way Osborn forgot what riches of faith, hope, and love everyone in the church can point to, especially those who were not healed and who had to find an answer *for that*.

Proud of God

Accordingly, we can be proud of the church, just so long as it's not a pride that can become fashionable—whether the criticism of today or the pride of yesterday. Legitimate boasting about the church doesn't say, "Really, that's some church, our church." Instead, it says, "Really, that's some God, our God!" Even the Babylonian Gilgamesh epic was acquainted with a similar song of praise: "Behold its outer wall, whose cornice is like copper! Peer at the inner wall, which none can equal. Seize upon the threshold, which is of old!" However, we know how all that ended, and we remember especially the proud word of Nebuchadnezzar: "Is not this great Babylon, which I have built by my mighty power as a royal residence and for the glory of my majesty?" (Dan. 4:30)! The language of our Psalm, however, issues into another king than any of this earth. That doesn't mean we must scrap all we've said as though suddenly it's less true. That wasn't true of the preceding Psalm either. We can put it this way—one is bound to the other. That's a familiar theme in the Psalms, one that maintains a needed self-confidence and boldness and pride. But everything is bound up with a needed confidence in God and a needed pride in God.

This God is still our God, even unto death. We've often ignored this, not realizing what this sudden mention of death has to do with it. As though death doesn't always come suddenly! As if the really glorious thing about our God isn't that He leads us to the most sudden, unexpected, and abrupt event there is—death! And, if He leads us even unto death, then He will not leave us in the lurch afterward. He will lead us still farther. We have only to look at Jesus Christ. Whose body has the church described herself to be if not His? And how else does He lead us even unto death and beyond if not through the church? That's how He leads us from cradle to grave. At both events the church is there—at baptism and at a funeral. The church is there with a song. That's how He leads us. To see what? To see the new Zion, the new Jerusalem.

The new Jerusalem

Is the church the new Zion, the New Jerusalem? No, we don't really hear about the church on the new earth. We hear of the New Jerusalem but not of the church.

Israel already knew something of this. Church and world were inseparably woven together in Israel. Indeed, we must admit that all we've heard in this Psalm has been spiritualized by us in a quite illegitimate way. That's why we intentionally left to the last how Zion points to the new Jerusalem, to stress one-sidedly what ought to bring us into the church. Since the days of the Old Testament, church and world are much more separated. We can regret this—that the church has become too spiritual and the world too worldly. Sometimes they no longer recognize each other. But we can also say something good about this—namely, that the church has always and rightly been afraid that it might prophesy inadequately, that what matters ultimately is not the church but the world—a more beautiful world, the original world and more, because world history has not been in vain. In the new Jerusalem "the honor of the nations" will be brought in (Rev. 21:26)! Talk about palaces! And of walking through them! How is it possible?

If this is so, what remains of the church's pride? This. The church has guarded as best it could the secret which the world doesn't understand, and has made this secret known as best it could—especially in this, that it was always its boast one day to outlive itself and to make itself superfluous.

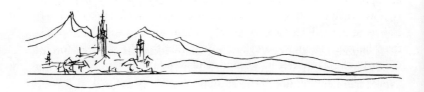

LIKE THE BEASTS

> *"Man cannot abide in his pomp,
> he is like the beasts that perish."*
>
> —Psalm 49:20

An important question when reading this picture about the transitoriness of life is the question whether the transitoriness described here simply goes with being human. When we read verse 17 we would incline toward an affirmative answer: "For when he dies he will carry nothing away; his glory will not go down after him." After all, what truth is more universal than that of verse 19: "he will go to the generation of his fathers"? The last expression is already familiar (cf. Gen. 25:8, 17, and Deut. 32:50). It represents that dying which is prepared for us all. Doesn't Ecclesiastes (3:21) ask concerning the fate of every man: "Who knows whether the spirit of man goes upward and the spirit of the beast goes down to the earth?" Is then the transitoriness of life, portrayed here in such "beastly" manner, universally human?

What a riddle that would be!

Apparently not, for that would be a riddle! This would not say enough, were it not for the fact that the poet asserts *that* riddle is now solved. The poet is not only a martyr but a prophet. He knows about riddles, and especially about an answer. Even in distress he can become so ecstatic about this that he reaches for his cither to put it into our hands and to disclose the mystery.

To what extent the transitoriness of life in general is simply part of life is a question we will let rest. We discussed that when dealing with Psalm 9. To be sure, we could say something more about it, for this Psalm suggests that something like a "ransom" is needed as the price of life if it's to be rescued from death. This can lead to the idea that death, even biological death, is not wholly self-explanatory in the Bible, that it is always seen in the context of guilt, as solder for sin (Rom. 6:23). Again, when reading Psalm 90, which is concerned with the transitoriness of life in general, we're struck by the fact that, after this transitoriness has been described in the first six verses, verse 7 speaks about our years passing under God's "wrath."

Be that as it may, transitoriness, as our Psalm portrays this in particular, the transitoriness that comes to a dead end, is not universally human nor does it touch everybody. After all, isn't this a Psalm about "the evil shepherd," describing a situation in which death leads people as a shepherd? That's in contrast to the Psalm about "the good shepherd" (Ps. 23) in which death is also present but not as a shepherd. There, at most, it's like a mine field through which the Lord who is my shepherd can lead me.

Not believing one's eyes

But, isn't this contradicted by what we just thought we heard the Preacher say in Ecclesiastes: "Who knows whether the spirit of man goes upward and the spirit of the beast goes down to the earth?"

The late Professor Aalders proposed an answer in his commentary which seems probable to me. He suggests that, by and large, when reading Ecclesiastes we must keep continually in mind that the Preacher speaks of what he *sees* and that this is not the same as what he *believes* or what *we* believe. In its anxious question, then, the quotation from the Preacher would call for faith in the opposite. "Who knows the difference between a man and an animal, when you come down to it?" This may then be read: "You wouldn't say there is any difference," but not to conclude: "there is none," but rather to conclude: "Yet there is a difference." A person simply can't believe his eyes!

I don't think it necessary—as Valeton does in his commentary on our Psalm—to see a deep rift between the Preacher and the Psalmist, even though it's significant that Valeton doesn't want to take the Psalm as a description of everyone's fate on earth. In any case, even this description rests upon a faith utterance. To turn it around, you wouldn't always say that man, with all his glory, can't hold his own and is simply like beasts that perish!

Two kinds of fate

In the Psalm as in our world all must die, the wise as well as fools (vs. 10). All abide in the power of Sheol (vs. 15), can take nothing with them, and all stand in the context of guilt (Ps. 90:7).

Yet this isn't all there is to say. There are those who, in addition, stand in the context of "uprightness" (vs. 14, R.S.V. margin). What this means is clear. It's the difference between those who also do good and those who only do themselves good (vs. 18), as we could say with a grim play on words. By this the former do not step out of the context of guilt, nor can they buy their own escape for "the ransom of their life is costly." Nonetheless, it's also true that God delivers them "from the power of Sheol"—or, which is the same thing—from the power of guilt. Even though they don't know how to hang the clapper they have heard the bell toll of Him who said He "came not to be served but to serve, and to give his life as a ransom for many" (Matt. 20:28). That is to say, they've heard of Him who, with all His glory and splendor, "did not count equality with God a thing to be grasped, but emptied himself, taking the form of a servant" (Phil. 2:6-7). They have heard this bell toll in such a way that something has changed in their life. The difference between doing good and doing themselves good, the difference between man and beast, has become evident in their existence. As for the others, how transitory is their dream of imperishableness, even if their deepest thought is that their houses shall always remain, and even if they name their lands for themselves. Böhl tells us that in an old Latin psalterium, the superscripture of Psalm 49 is *"Vox ecclesiae super Lazaro et divite purpurato.* That is to say, according to church tradition this psalm deals with the difference between the poor Lazarus and the rich man clad in purple after death. Indeed, in the parable of the poor Lazarus (Luke 16:19f) the ideas that are already present in the psalm *in nuce* are worked out." But what church, when reading this today, dare think only of two different *persons* and isn't obliged to to beyond this to see a comparison between two different climates and cultures, to see the difference between the poor East and the rich West? Surely the church will have to do this if it wants to stay "upright" in any sense of the word. That's what the Psalm wants us to be—unless we want to be like the beasts that perish when we die.

Like the beasts?

Perhaps we've busied ourselves too much and too quickly with the ultimate fate of man and moved too quickly from today to the last day. Possibly the poet, when he thought of death, wasn't thinking of the end of life that everyone awaits, but of a deadly danger into which the oppressor of the present has brought him. Undoubtedly when he speaks of the "morning" in which the upright will rule over the braggards (vs. 14), he doesn't think directly of what we now call the last day, but simply of the morning when the present danger is over and when the "big shots" have had it. Such things happen day after day, thank God. We think of the day when Herod "put on his royal robes, took his seat on the throne, and made an oration" to the people who shouted, "The voice of a god . . . !" Then we read: "Immediately an angel of the Lord smote him, because he did not give God the glory; and he was eaten by worms and died" (Acts 12:21-23).

Meantime, it remains a fact that there are people who are not like the beasts that perish because their life is not like the beasts (1 Tim. 5:18). If only we don't do the beasts an injustice by this comparison! God is concerned not only with the perishing of people. He is also concerned with animals (Jonah 4:11).

PROJECTING

Our text raises an important question. In the Bible we read that God created man in His own image, that man is a thought of God, a dream of God. Today—and not only today—we ask whether the reverse is not more likely to be the case. Suppose God did not create man in His image but that man created God in his image and that God is man's thought and man's dream, his greatest and most needed dream perhaps, but still a dream? We can see this clearly in the gods of the heathen, gods who manifested such terribly human form and even mischievous human traits. But we must not suppose that the God of the Bible will be spared such criticism. In the communist East German Republic a book is distributed among youth as a sort of communist profession of faith gift. It's written by a number of professors, but in very understandable language for anyone at all interested. It aims to give a complete interpretation of world events, and is called *Universe, Earth, Man*. It's a big book but devotes only a few pages to the world of the gods and of God. Religion means protection of property, exploitation, and falsehood. It's not even the best but one of the worst dreams of mankind, a vanquished point of view. Once people needed it to fill in the dark places on the map of their knowing and doing in order to make it a bit less terrifying. Now we know so much that we can say confidently that

modern technology has made all gods and the God of Israel an-
tique aids, a mere projection. Is that true of God the Father, to
whom we speak and pray continually? Yes, it's true of Him too.
What else is He but a gigantic enlargment of my own father?
Wouldn't it be nice if He gave us exactly what we want! To suppose that what Christians want to exist would still exist—that's all
too supicious, too good to be true (Freud).

Don't be afraid of it

What shall we say about this? We might begin humorously by
saying what this God of whom people say He needs us to exist
says about it. He says that He's *not* hungry (vs. 12)!

Of course, we must go into it more deeply. And we must not
be afraid. If God has created us in His image, then we're also
permitted also to create Him a bit in our own image. We're somewhat alike. We look a bit like each other. That's no reason to be
afraid. On the contrary, it's something for which we can be very
glad.

Moreover, the fact that we can see a heavenly Fatherhood via
an earthly fatherhood doesn't alter the fact that the latter may be
dependent upon the former (Eph. 3:15).

No wonder that we believe this God hears our prayer, sometimes even literally and precisely as we thought and dreamed, and
that He answers as Someone said who knew Him very well: "Just
ask!" (Matt. 21:22).

That God should come so close to us and that His answers
should correspond to and fit our questions is no proof of His absence but rather points to a very particular presence. In the same
way, the humanity of God doesn't argue against but rather for this
presence. Else one would have no idea what grace is—and, indeed, atheism has no idea of this.

Something to be afraid of

However, we should be a bit concerned about it and frightened
by it—and perhaps a great deal. Projecting, imagining something

about God, is permissible. Surely faith may do this, just as faith can imagine endlessly without necessarily running wild. But not all projecting is permissible, and not all imagination is good. Projection can also be done in an appalling manner. We're all familiar with the story (Exod. 32) in which people thought about God but worshiped a calf! Again, people may think that God is white—at least more white than black. Or that God is Western—at least more Western than Eastern. Adults may think that God is on the side of adults—at least more on their side than on the side of youth. Youth may think that God is on the side of youth—at least more on their side than on the side of adults. If I have a quarrel with my wife, I may think God is on my side—at least more on my side than on hers.

So everybody is inclined to think that God is the first and most clever and sophisticated member of *his* party. Representations of God arise that are so obvious, so based on self-interest, so much a dream of our own self-centeredness that suddenly and frighteningly atheistic propaganda becomes correct. That's something to be afraid of! Whether we now serve a golden calf or contribute to our propaganda, the one is not more godless than the other.

The second commandment

Who can keep us from these false representations of God and from these appalling projections? Who is the one we cannot get along without? Who else but the God of the Bible? Who has forbidden those things we've just described more sharply and scathingly than He did in the second commandment? The house of Jeroboam, which excelled in idol worship, literally goes to the dogs (1 Kings 14:11). How threatening is our text: "you thought that I was one like yourself"!

To whom is this spoken? It's spoken to the "faithful ones" (vs. 5), to people who "recite" God's statutes and dream about them. It's addressed to people who have His covenant "on their lips" and who never stop taking about God and religion (vs. 16). It's spoken to believers of the first rank, to people who exalt God in a very special way. But, according to our Psalm, it's a god who

shields thievery and adultery and fraternal strife. The true God refuses to play the role of the great Thief (Is the god of capitalism
out of date?). The true God refuses to play the role of the great
Adulterer (Is being in league with brute force out of date?). The
true God even refuses to play the role of the great Schismatic (Is
it out of date to represent God as the special God of my church
and less or not at all the God of other churches?). It might be the
god of a particular kind of orthodoxy against whom the God of
our Psalm carries on, a dead orthodoxy against which James carries on, a god in whom even devils can believe, and thus a devilish god (James 2:19)—the god of a dead faith and of dead
works, an abstract God without neighbor. God refuses to be like
that. God without the neighbor is simply unthinkable! It's disturbing to note that those who in verse 5 are hailed as "faithful ones"
and who in verse 16 are portrayed as people who want to exalt
His name can be called "wicked" in the same verse and as those
"who forget God" in verse 22.

Reasonable worship

One can imagine the God of our Psalm saying to people, "No,
I don't look very much like you," and He might add, "Wouldn't it
be better if you looked a little more like Me?" And we can add
what we read in verse 14, that, in the end, we must pay our vows
to Him. Then we'll look like Him who never has done anything
but keep His vows and maintain His covenant faithfulness and
follow His neighbor in the costly manner of John 3:16: "For God
so loved the world that he gave his only Son."

To pay our vows and offerings to the Most High, to make good
our commitments to Him, to translate our good intentions into
deeds, cost what it may (a sacrifice)—what else is this but to
make good our commitments to the neighbor, to translate our
good intentions into deeds at home, at work, or wherever? At any
rate, in Romans 12:1, Paul says that "this is your rational worship" (Goodspeed). That's what true worship is—to have God on
our lips and to dream of His statutes. An inescapable bond between our relation to the Most High and our relation to our

neighbor appears irrefutable in the way in which the offered sacrifices are directed *against* the thievery, adultery, lovelessness, and fraternal strife which have already been mentioned. Anyone who thinks he can drive a wedge between one and the other thinks too facilely of God and makes himself a god, a neighborless god—and that's a preposterous projection which has to be called godless because it's neighborless. Accordingly, this Psalm teaches us to think of godlessness not first in the East German Republic but to look for it closer home, in our own hearts.

A pure image

Fortunately we have one image that doesn't deceive us. We have one wholly pure image of God, Jesus Christ. Once our little daughter said jauntily at table, "I know God's name." We were curious, of course, and asked for her answer. She said, "Jesus." Indeed. He is as like His Father as "two peas in a pod." Only He can keep us from our shameful projections. To be sure, He says, "Ask, and it will be given you," but He concludes that passage beginning "Ask what you want," by saying: "So whatever you wish that men would do to you, do so to them; for this is the law and the prophets" (Matt. 7:7, 12). For a long time we thought that the last verse short-circuited the rest until we came to the fruitful insight (N. H. Ridderbos) that the one is bound to the other. "Just ask," Jesus says, "in the sphere of love for neighbor what you need in order to love." While that's not the only sphere where we may ask (Matt. 21:22), He sees to it that our projections in every case must be confronted with this if they are to reach their goal.

Why we need God

Now we know why we need God. First of all, so that we can come to our neighbor. Second, where this isn't possible, so that we may come to forgiveness (vs. 15)! Third, in so doing, to get away from myself, away from inevitable self-conceit.

Let's go back to where we began. Do we believe in God out of fear and need? I don't know why we should be ashamed of that! Without meaning anything different, I'd rather answer the question why I believe by saying that I believe in God because of my neighbor, out of fear for my neighbor. I believe if for no other reason than that I can't help my neighbor by myself.

If for no other reason. Now we dare say more. In the gospel it's not only about my neighbor, though some try to tell us this nowadays. It's also for my sake (Phil. 2:4). I'm not wholly taken up with my neighbor because God isn't. In the worship of life there's also "an element of extravagance—thought, time, money are squandered which could have been used more 'usefully'" (Herngreen on Matthew 26:9). We need God not only for the sake of our neighbor but also for the true concern for ourselves and also for the true disinterestedness. He is our greatest profit and our very greatest luxury.

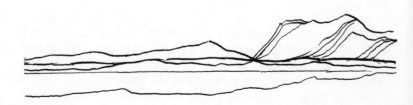